IN THEIR
OWN WORDS
2

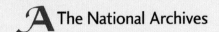
The National Archives

IN THEIR OWN WORDS

2

More letters from history

CONWAY

LONDON · OXFORD · NEW YORK · NEW DELHI · SYDNEY

CONWAY

Bloomsbury Publishing Plc
50 Bedford Square, London, WC1B 3DP, UK

BLOOMSBURY, CONWAY and the Conway logo
are trademarks of Bloomsbury Publishing Plc

The National Archives logo © Crown Copyright 2018
The National Archives logo is a trade mark of The National Archives
and is used under licence.

First published in Great Britain 2018

ISBN: HB: 978-1-8448-6522-2;
         ePDF: 978-1-8448-6524-6;
         eBook: 978-1-8448-6523-9

2 4 6 8 10 9 7 5 3 1

Page design by Nicola Liddiard, Nimbus Design
Printed and bound in China by C&C Offset Printing Co.

Bloomsbury Publishing Plc makes every effort to ensure that
the papers used in the manufacture of our books are natural,
recyclable products made from wood grown in well-managed forests.
Our manufacturing processes conform to the environmental
regulations of the country of origin.

To find out more about our authors and books visit
www.bloomsbury.com and sign up for our newsletters

Contents

Expeditions, foreign policy and espionage

Conflict, unrest and protest

Relations and relationships

Art, science and popular culture

Introduction

Before literacy, people relied on storytelling, singing and oral tradition to retell events and preserve their culture. News was passed by word of mouth, often becoming embellished or distorted as centuries passed. The first written letter to be recorded dates back to around 500 BC; it is said to have been written by a Persian queen. Egyptian papyrus was the most popular writing material in the early days of written communication, but its shortage caused other mediums to be developed, such as bark from trees and parchment and vellum form cured animal skins.

We know that paper was being used in Dunhuang, China by AD 150. As early as the tenth century, paper made from cotton came to the West from the Far East; by the twelfth century it was commonly used in the West. By 1500, paper-making and printing were firmly established in Southern Europe. The advent of steam-driven paper-making machines in the nineteenth century, which could make paper with fibres from wood pulp, opened up new possibilities. Reading and writing letters became an accessible means of corresponding and recording and therefore learning to read and write became a necessity. Letter writing became a way of life, essential for maintaining long-distance relationships, for recording laws and literature, for having a voice.

When we look back through history, it's easy to forget that literacy is a recent skill. The ability to read and write was scarce in medieval times. Learning this skill must have appeared to many at the time as something of a revelation, not dissimilar to the invention of email. In the past, when face to face was the only method of communication, the ability to write letters became a vital way of recording information. People were able to stay in touch with families, businesses could negotiate trade deals and religious leaders were able to pass on their teaching more widely. Explorers sought to pack in as much detail as they could in their correspondence in order to inform the recipient of discoveries and behaviours of indigenous peoples. As communication beyond the twentieth century becomes more sophisticated, letter writing has become less common. In this second series of collections of letters from The National Archives, we go back in time to explore the thoughts and words of people across an extensive period of time.

This collection crosses many borders. It brings us voices from the past, allows us to enter the minds of historical figures and lesser-known characters with great stories to tell. The book includes all kinds of letters covering topics from forbidden love to indecent conduct and from well-known historical events to lesser-known adventures.

The book covers a wide range of subjects. Read how King John brags to his mother, Eleanor of Aquitaine, about how well things are working out for him, perhaps an oblique reference to his murder of his own nephew, Arthur of Brittany. Discover how surprisingly engaging Raisa Gorbacheva's conversation with the Minister of Agriculture is, on the topic of potato recipes in Belarus. Equally we are able to get an insight into the relationship Mikhail Gorbachev had with Margaret Thatcher: upon hearing of her resignation, he wrote to her with a quality of friendly familiarity. And familiarity fuses with formality in the expert letter-writing skills of Abraham Lincoln where, in a beautifully hand-scripted letter to Queen Victoria, he congratulates her on the news of the Prince of Wales's wedding to Princess Alexandra of Denmark.

Letters written by prominent figures in history, especially when in their own hand, give us an impression of eavesdropping into something private; we get an insight into the character of Richard III in a letter written in his own hand, when he vents his anger at his disloyal nobles. Nelson Mandela's letter of thanks to an anonymous admirer gives us a deeper understanding of his optimism as he signs off as an 'awaiting trial prisoner'; Gandhi's letter to Sir Stafford Cripps demonstrates how tension in writing can be achieved in only three short words 'something is wrong'; and three short words used by Elizabeth I tell us of the special relationship she has with her step-mother, Katherine Parr, when she signs herself as 'most humble daughter'.

Correspondence from ordinary people of their time gives us no less exciting vision into a world past. Full of detail and colour, excitement and horror, an explorer's letter uncovers a story of survival in the wilds of Timbuctoo where a violent tale of tribal encounters and robbery brings to the imagination how dangerous such voyages were. And yet the excitement of the prospect of new discoveries is evident in a young botanist's letter, when after finally seeking consent from his father, he accepts his place on the *Beagle* and embarks on a five year voyage to explore the flora and fauna of foreign lands. The emigration to Canada of a father's 'two little girls', whom he cannot care for, forces us to consider issues around poverty, colonisation and social history of the time.

Written letters are becoming a rarity. These chosen letters from The National Archives are part of a treasurable collection, offering us glimpses into people's thoughts and lives. We are fortunate that many letters still survive to be discovered, especially from a distant past. They give us a better understanding of history and empower us to use our imaginations and draw our own conclusions. They allow us to delve into and debate the thoughts of people who were of the time, literary, extraordinary and insightful.

Drunkenness,
debauchery
and dark dealings

Imposter or long-lost son?
The Tichborne case

1870s

The 1870s saw one of the longest-running and most sensational legal disputes in British history. It involved the 'claimant', who declared himself to be the presumed-dead Sir Roger Tichborne, heir of a wealthy baronet. Lady Tichborne was certain that the claimant was her son, even though he was shorter, much fatter, and could no longer speak French, despite having been fluent in the past. Other members of the family disagreed. The story caught the public's imagination, resulting in songs, plays, newspapers and souvenirs and, in 1978, a film.

In April 1854 a twenty-one-year-old Sir Roger Tichborne boarded the *Bella* for the West Indies, but the ship never reached her destination. Lady Tichborne, however, would not believe her son was dead and on 5 August 1865 an advert appeared in the *Australasian* newspaper offering a reward for the person who could discover his fate. The description in the advert stated that Sir Roger would be 'about 32 years of age, of delicate constitution, rather tall, with very light brown hair and blue eyes'.

In 1866, Lady Tichborne received news from Australia that Sir Roger was still alive. The person who was claiming to be the Tichborne heir was a butcher who lived in Wagga Wagga, between Sydney and Melbourne, and went by the name of Tom Castro.

After meeting the claimant in Paris in 1867, Lady Tichborne asserted that he was indeed her son. Other people also came forward to support his claim, although many expressed concerns. An examination of the case in the Court of Chancery was undertaken in 1868, which was followed by civil proceedings in 1871 and then a criminal trial in 1873. The claimant was found guilty of perjury and decreed to be Arthur Orton, originally from Wapping, and went on to serve ten years of a fourteen-year sentence. As a result of the trials he had become a form of celebrity, but in 1898 he ultimately died a poor man.

As a final twist to the story, the Tichborne family agreed to a plate marked 'Sir Roger Charles Doughty Tichborne' being present on the claimant's coffin. There has, however, remained some doubt as to Castro's true identity.

On 24 July 1866, the claimant wrote this letter to Lady Tichborne while still in Australia. The first of many, it provides an interesting insight into their relationship. In his opening sentence the claimant expresses his disappointment that Lady

Sir Roger Tichborne.

The Tichborne claimant.

Tichborne did not acknowledge him as her son in her previous letter. He then confidently states: 'surely my dear mama you must know my writing'. Assuming that they would soon meet, the claimant attempts to explain away the difference in stature between himself and the twenty-one-year-old Sir Roger by disclosing: 'I enjoy much good health. I have grown very stout.' Lady Tichborne did not have access to much money herself but the claimant puts financial pressure on her to fund his trip back to England, lamenting the possibility of never seeing her again unless the money can be raised. After writing 'dear mama' in his letter four times, reinforcing the supposed relationship between them, the claimant signs off: 'I Remain your affectionate son Roger Charles Tichborne'.

The Tichborne Claimant Trial, judges and jury, 1873.

No 4

Sydney July 24 /65

My Dear Mama

I received your letter yesterday morning. And was somewhat disapointed. that you do not Acknowledge me has your son Surely my dear mama you must Know my writing. You have cause me a deal of trouble. But it matters not Has I have no wish to leave the Country ware I enjoy such good health I have grown very stout. Yesterday one of Uncle Edwards Old servants call on me. he been living here a long while. He is name Giutfogle. you must remember him. He was remodelling the Garden at Tichborne when I was staying at Uncle Edwards

He knew me has soon
has he see me. His wife was
with him. she look very young
yet. And yet she has eleven
children. You spoke of Bangle
in your letter to Cubbit.
I have made enquires but can
not find him. Mr Turnel is
here with Sir John Young.
I have seen him. And had
a long conversation with him
. I heard that the Rev Pattes phillips
was out here. but I can not
find him. My Dear Mama the
post closes in two minutes more
for France so I will say good
bye. incase I am too late. If to
late i will send this to England
has the English Mail does not
close for two hours after the
the Mail for France

I have enclose a photograph of my self that you may see how greatly I have improve Hoping my dear mama to see alive once more. But I am afraid not, has I can not get surficient money to come home with. Good bye my dear mama and may the Blesed Marie have mercy on your soul.

I Remain your Affectionate Son
Roger Charles Tichborne

Metropolitan Hotel
Pitts Street
Sydney

To Lady Tichborne
40 rue neuve des Mathurins

Sydney July 24 1866

My Dear Mama

I received your letter yesterday morning and was somewhat disappointed that you do not acknowledge me has your son, surely my Dear mama you must know my writing. You have cause(d) me a deal of trouble. But it matters not has I have no wish to leave a country where I have enjoyed much good health. I have grown very stout. Yesterday one of Uncle Edward's old servants call(ed) on me, he been living here a long while. He is name(d) Guilfoyle, you must remember him. He was remodeling the Garden at Tichborne when I was staying at Uncle Edward's.

He knew me has soon has he see me. His wife was with him. She look(ed) very young _____ and yet she has eleven children. You spoke of Bogle in your letter to Cubbit I have made enquiries but can not find him. Mr Turvel is here with Sir John Young. I have seen him and had a long conversation with him. I heard that the Rev father's Phillips was out here but I can not find him. My Dear Mama the post closes in ten minutes more for France so I will say good bye in case I am too late. If to(o) late I will send this to England has the English mail does not close for two hours after the mail for France.

I have enclosed a photograph of my self that you may see how greatly I have emprove(d). Hoping my Dear mama to see alive once more. But I am afraid not has I can not get suficience money to come home with. Good bye my Dear mama and may the Blessed Maria have mercy on your soul.

        I Remain your
          affectionate son
            Roger Charles Tichborne

              Metropolitan Hotel
              Pitts street
              Sydney

T. Lady Tichborne
40 Rue Neuve des Mathurins

Suffragette struggles with authority
Hilda Burkett and Florence Tunks and the Bath Hotel case

1914

The fight for equal parliamentary franchise for men and women was long, arduous and fraught with tensions. It was not until 1918 that some women were granted the right to vote in parliamentary elections and another decade before they could vote on the same terms as men. During this struggle some women chose militant tactics instead of constitutional campaigning.

In April 1914, Hilda Burkett (also sometimes spelled 'Burkitt' who also had the alias 'Hilda Byron') and Florence Tunks were arrested for setting fire to the Bath Hotel in Felixstowe. This was not the first time that Hilda had been arrested for the cause: she had previously been imprisoned, during which time she had refused food, and in 1909 had been the first suffragette prisoner to be force-fed. At the time of the attack on the Bath Hotel, Hilda was evading rearrest under the 1913 Prisoners (Temporary Discharge for Ill-health) Act – commonly called the 'Cat and Mouse' Act – which meant that hunger-striking prisoners who became too ill from force-feeding to remain in prison could be temporarily released until they were well enough to resume their sentence.

As a result of other attacks that had occurred a few days previously and were reportedly carried out by two women, the police began their investigation by looking for women who had been absent from their lodgings on the night of the fire. The search led them to Burkett and Tunks' lodgings, where they discovered the equipment the women would have needed to carry out the arson attack.

After being arrested, Burkett wrote to a friend asking them to let her father know that she was in prison. She writes that she thinks the police will find it difficult to prove her involvement in the attack and that she suspects she will be found not guilty. This is something that the police seem also to have feared: in a letter to the Home Office the chief constable of East Suffolk Police wrote that 'actual evidence against these women will be very difficult to place properly before the Court'.

Hilda also writes in her letter that she has not revealed her true identity since being arrested and asks that any responses sent to her do not give this away. This caution came too late, however, though it would not be letters addressed to her while in prison that would reveal her secret. In his letter to the Home Office, housed in the same document as Hilda's, the chief constable of East Suffolk Police wrote that they had

HOTEL BURNED DOWN.

BARE AND BLACKENED WALLS.

"NO PEACE TILL WOMEN GET THE VOTE."

The evening papers on Tuesday stated that the Bath Hotel, Felixstowe, was burned down that morning by Suffragettes. The hotel occupied a commanding site on the Felixstowe cliffs.

The fire was first discovered by the coastguards at the wireless station at Felixstowe. The fire brigade were at once summoned, but before their arrival the fire had secured a firm hold, and within two hours the whole of the building had been gutted.

Attached to the trees at the corner of the building were a number of ordinary tie-on labels bearing such inscriptions as "No peace until women get the vote," "Votes for women," etc.

There was no one in the hotel at the time. The furnishing of it for the visitors' season, however, had just been completed, and the damage is estimated at £35,000.

At twenty minutes past eleven the debris was still smouldering. Nothing whatever had been saved, and only the bare and blackened walls are left standing.

The hotel comprised fifty-five sitting and bed-rooms, dining-rooms, smoking-roofs, and lounges.

Two Women Arrested.

Later in the day two women, both of whom refused to give their names, and who were apparently strangers to the district, were arrested in Felixstowe. They were brought before the magistrate the following day and were remanded until May 9. They were taken to Ipswich Gaol.

been able to positively identify Burkett and Tunks from letters addressed to the women found in their lodgings. In May the women were found guilty and sentenced to two years' imprisonment, and transferred from Ipswich prison to Holloway.

In his letter the police chief also wrote that although the women had refused to have their fingerprints taken, they had been photographed and copies had been sent to the Metropolitan Police. In addition to requiring the police to fingerprint and photograph suffrage prisoners, the Home Office also kept a card index of suffragettes so that they could keep track of them and cross-reference offences. Compiled between 1906 and 1914, the index lists 1,333 names: 1,224 women and 109 men.

Prominent suffragettes Annie Kenny and Christabel Pankhurst holding a 'Votes for Women' placard, 1906.

When looking at the index entries of Hilda Burkett and Florence Tunks, we can see that the Felixstowe fire was the last suffrage outrage that they committed. This could be in part because in August 1914 there was an amnesty of suffrage prisoners: many women's suffrage societies had suspended activities at the outbreak of war and in return the Home Office organised the release of prisoners. Most women were released promptly, but it was not until September that Hilda was freed, perhaps prompted by a petition she had sent to the Home Office in which she wrote that she had been force-fed for the duration of her incarceration.

Just before her release, Hilda allegedly promised not to carry out any future militant attacks. Despite this, however, it is impossible to guess whether, if war had not broken out and campaigning had not been suspended, Hilda Burkett would have continued with militant tactics to obtain votes for women.

~ 38412
691A

Copy of a letter written by Suffragette prisoner
No. 135 — Byron.

〰〰〰〰

Dear Fred

I want you to kindly pass this letter on
to father. I promised I would let him know
if ever I was arrested. It seems anyone who
is a Suffragette is liable to arrest any time.

Dear Father

I cannot send the letter directly to you
as I have refused to give my name or say anything about myself. I was arrested on Tuesday
at about 1 pm. on suspicion of having caused
a fire at Felixstowe, but of course they have
to prove things, this I think they will find
impossible, so I hope to get off. At present I
am on remand till Friday May 8th it seems
a long time doesn't it. Ofcourse I am not
taking food or water, what will be the result
I do not know. I am quite prepared to give my
life if need be, but I suppose McKenna will
desire that. The Police have seized all my
luggage, money, bicycle, but I presume I
shall get it back when they have pawed
everything over. If you look at the papers
you will no doubt see how my case goes
on. If you write be careful what you say
as if I can keep my identity from the officials
I shall certainly do so.

With much love to everyone & yourself
Your loving daughter
Ola

Addressed to
F.G. Wood Esq.
93 Francis Road
Erdington
Birmingham.

Copy of a letter written by suffragette prisoner
no.135 — Byron

Dear Fred

    I want you to kindly pass this letter on to
father. I promised I would let him know if ever I
was arrested. It seems anyone who is a Suffragette
is liable to arrest any time.

Dear Father

    I cannot send the letter directly to you as
I have refused to give my name or say anything
about myself. I was arrested on Tuesday at
about 1pm on suspicion of having caused a fire
at Felixstowe but of course they have to prove
things, this I think they will find impossible, so
I hope to get off. At present I am on remand till
Friday May 8th, it seems a long time doesn't it.
Of course I am not taking food or water, what will
be the effect I do not know. I am quite prepared
to give my life if need be, but I suppose McKenna
will decide that. The Police have seized all my
luggage, money, bicycle, but I presume I shall get
it back when they have pawed everything over. If
you look at the papers you will no doubt see how
my case goes on. If you write be careful what you
say as if I can keep my identity from the officials
I shall certainly do so.

    With much love to everyone & yourself
                            Your loving daughter
                                Ola

Addressed to
  F.G. Wood Esq.
    93 Francis Road
        Erdington
          Birmingham.

Calling time on drunkards
A plea for action against the George Inn

One of the early casualties of the First World War was, in many respects, the community pub or, more accurately, the liberal consumption of alcohol on licensed premises. Before the outbreak of war, and partly because of the rising support of the temperance movement, urging the moderate consumption of alcohol, licensing laws began to restrict the opening hours of premises. This was taken a step further immediately after the outbreak of war in August 1914, when Parliament passed the Defence of the Realm Act, which covered a range of measures to support the Allied effort of the war. A section of the Act looked specifically at the hours during which publicans could sell alcohol, as it was strongly believed that high levels of alcohol consumption would have a negative impact on the war effort. It therefore restricted opening hours for licensed premises to lunch (noon–2pm) and later to supper (6.30–9.30pm).

However, even with these changes in force, the British government became increasingly concerned about how the high levels of alcohol consumption still threatened the productivity of the war effort and good work ethics. If anything, consumption was increasing because in many cases wages were rising, particularly for those in industries vital to war, such as shipbuilding, as overtime became the norm. A campaign to persuade people to consume less alcohol led by the Chancellor of the Exchequer, David Lloyd George, had little effect, so in October 1915 the British government announced a further series of measures they believed would reduce alcohol consumption further. A 'No Treating Order' laid down that any drink ordered was to be paid for by the person supplied, in order to dissuade people from buying rounds of drinks or drinks on credit. The maximum penalty for defying the government order was six months' imprisonment.

In addition, the government became increasingly concerned about the increase in alcohol consumption in specific areas of the country vital to the war effort. An enormous cordite munitions factory built to supply ammunition to British forces had been established in the town of Gretna, just over the Scottish border, twelve miles north of the English city of Carlisle, employing more than 15,000 workers. Although most of the workers were well behaved, the cases of drunkenness and antisocial behaviour, and resulting convictions, quadrupled. There was also a heightened risk of hampering the war effort through increased sick absences and the threat of serious accidents as workers had to manually handle nitroglycerine and guncotton into cordite paste, and load the matter into shell cases.

In June 1916, in a decision involving both central government and the local authorities, the newly formed Central Control Board took control of five local breweries and 363 licensed premises covering 300 square miles, including parts of north and west Cumberland, south-west Scotland, and the city of Carlisle, 'for the duration of the war and twelve months thereafter'. The scheme became known as the Carlisle Experiment and the aim of it was to control the drinking habits of individuals without resorting to restricting personal liberty.

The Board acted quickly, closing nearly forty per cent of public houses by 1917 and revoking all off-sales licences. All advertising referring to alcohol was illegal and a ban was placed on the display of liquor bottles in windows. Within the state-owned public houses (many of which remained state-owned until 1971), strict opening hours were enforced, and the managers became government employees on a fixed salary and were offered no inducement to increase alcohol sales (in fact, commissions were given for the sale of non-alcoholic drinks and food only). The sale of food was actively encouraged and 'snug' bars were repurposed as eating areas. Pubs were made to be attractive to women and families and table service was introduced. Drinks' prices were fixed by the state, to avoid competition between the different pubs, and the sale of 'chasers' – spirits accompanying beer – was banned. The only beer to be served was that brewed by the local, government-owned brewery. This was brewed at a reduced level of alcohol or was, effectively, watered down. Furthermore, it was also prohibited to serve alcohol to people under the age of eighteen, as was the selling of spirits on Saturdays.

In this atmosphere of restraint, the George Inn in the village of Warwick Bridge, just five miles west of Carlisle, was opened in the spring of 1918 in the hope that the new licensee would bring some order to proceedings with the support of the Board and the local constabulary. However, as we can see from the letter to the Board written by an 'onlooker' on 29 November 1919, this was far from the case, though this was not fully corroborated by an inspector's visit on 5 December 1919.

Mr Saunders   Warwick Bridge
Dear Sir   Nov 29th 1919

Are you aware how the
George in Conducted it as been
very loosely Conducted ever since
Miss Byshop came but getting worse
last Saturday night it was most
disgusting the low language that
was used in the House and the
blackguardish songs which was
Sung and she just stands and laughs
at it instead of stopping it but she
is very often half drunk hersef there
is a Certain Class goes to her House
Can get a drink any time and get
small quanties out in bottles as well
and then you advertise what the
Control as done but you should
advertise at same time how loosely
some of your Houses is Conducted
the PC on Corby Hill dare not
interfere as he goes there for so much
drink at one time they used to pitch
Corks into a Pint for drinks one night
they raffled a Watch and there is 2
men goes to the House and takes

Mrs Saunders

Warwick Bridge

November 29th 1919

Are you aware how the George in [sic] is conducted it as [sic] been very loosely conducted ever since Mrs Hyslop came but getting worse. Last Saturday night it was most disgusting the low language that was used in the House and the blackguardish songs which was sung and she just stands and laughs at it instead of stopping it but she is very often half drunk herself. There is a certain class goes to her house can get drunk any time and get small quantities out in bottles as well and then you advertise what the control was done but you should advertise at same time how loosely some of your Houses is conducted. The PC on Corby Hill dare not interfere as he goes there for so much drink at one time they used to pitch corks into a pint for drinks one night they raffled a watch and there is 2 men goes to the House and takes bets for Horse Racing. It is a country talk how the George is conducted and what I see and hear I will believe and I think it was time it was put a stop to or reported to higher quarters

Yours onlooker

Police 'sting' operations against clairvoyants
Sir Arthur Conan Doyle's defence of spiritualism

1920s

Famed for his creation of perhaps the best-known consulting detective in the history of literature, Sir Arthur Conan Doyle was a superstar author of his time. However, as well as being the genius behind Sherlock Holmes, Conan Doyle had many other interests, which he pursued with a passion equal to that felt by the legions of fans of his masterful fictional creation. These included his profession in medicine, his campaigning for body armour for men serving in the First World War, and his passion for spiritualism. If ever there was a man with many strings to his bow, then he was certainly one.

At the time he wrote this particular letter in the 1920s, Conan Doyle was a prominent public figure with a reputation for campaigning. He had a long-standing interest in spiritualism, which prompted him to write in defence of the work of mediums at a time when police and the authorities were attempting to clamp down on fraudulent clairvoyants and their activities. This letter shows Conan Doyle's distaste of 'sting' operations being carried out by the police against clairvoyants and demonstrates his concern that evidence was submitted so that those 'well-intentioned persons' would not be unfairly prosecuted.

Sir Arthur Conan Doyle

It says much about the standing and fame of Conan Doyle that he felt able to address the Home Secretary directly on the matter, and the file from which this letter comes shows how seriously his comments were taken by the government since it contains correspondence between officials that examine closely the police operations to which Conan Doyle refers. He was indeed correct in his reference to the sting operations and there are detailed police reports into the covert investigations conducted by undercover female police officers seeking the services of clairvoyants. The reports cover everything from how the clairvoyants were contacted to descriptions of their homes and their predictions for the future of each woman.

It is interesting to think that although it was Conan Doyle who prompted this gathering of information by government officials, he would never have had access to any of the material in the file: he would simply have received a response that would probably have been drafted by a government official on behalf of the Home Secretary.

This letter is only one of a number of documents in the collection of The National Archives that deal with Conan Doyle's interest in spiritualism. Others include letters of support for particular mediums, as well as a petition he signed addressed to King George V regarding the unfair treatment of clairvoyants. It is somewhat strange to think that earlier on in his career, and through his greatest literary creation, Conan Doyle was concerned with science and deduction, while his interests later in life focused very much on what could be considered the ethereal world.

4496

THE PSYCHIC BOOK SHOP AND LIBRARY,

(PROPRIETOR: SIR ARTHUR CONAN DOYLE).

*"EVERY PSYCHIC STUDENT SHOULD HAVE
HIS OWN LIBRARY, HOWEVER SMALL."*

ABBEY HOUSE,

VICTORIA STREET,

WESTMINSTER, LONDON, S.W.

(OPPOSITE DEAN'S YARD).

449636

Sir

May I, with all respect, draw your attention to the leader in the "Morning Post" and the letter in the "Daily Express" expressing disapproval of the prosecution of clairvoyants or mediums.

Granting that the public need some protection against imposters should it not be left to the public to invoke the law. At present there is no demand for protection but the mediums are attacked by police men or women who pretend to be mourners, incite the offence which the law condemns, and then in many cases share the fines which the law imposes. Surely such a use of self interested "agents-provocateurs" cannot be Justified.

Hoping that you will give the matter your attention

Yours faithfully

Arthur Conan Doyle.

Oct 17. /25.

Sir

    May I, with all respect, draw your attention to the leader in the "Morning Post" and the letter in the "Daily Express" expressing disapproval of the persecution of clairvoyants or mediums.

    Granting that the public need some protection against imposters it should not be left to the public to invoke the law. At present there is no demand for protection but the mediums are attacked by policemen or women who produce a summons, incite the offence which the law condemns, and then in many cases share the fines which the law imposes. Surely such a use of self interested "agents-provocateurs" cannot be justified.

    Hoping that you will give the matter your attention.

      Yours faithfully

        Arthur Conan Doyle

Dealing with 'offensive litter'
Calls to moderate indecency in 'Jekyll-and-Hyde' Park

1931

In 1923, the London Council for the Promotion of Public Morality – formed in 1899 to combat vice and indecency – took it upon itself to assess the prevalence of 'improper and indecent conduct' in the Royal Parks. Their report, submitted to HM Office of Works, claimed sightings of 746 cases of impropriety in Hyde Park over ten nights of observation. The news prompted the *Daily Sketch* to quip that 'Hyde Park should be renamed Jekyll-and-Hyde Park, for like the Robert Louis Stevenson character, it appears to have a dual personality'.

The department was already by this point quite conscious of what was going on in one of London's most revered green spaces. 'The question of immorality in Hyde Park is one which is constantly before this Department' stated MP Harry E Brittain in the House of Commons in July 1922. Approximately 350 acres in size, the areas of the park unlit by lights from the pathways were proving to be fruitful spots for couples with nowhere else to go. 'One has only to walk through Hyde Park at almost any hour to see couples not only lying cuddled up, but actually lying on top of each other' exclaimed a reverend from South Acton. 'This is now so usual that they do not wait for darkness to fall but do it in broad daylight. I had a walk through Hyde Park last week, and the sights to be seen near Marble Arch are disgusting.'

The problem of solving the situation was causing the police a considerable amount of grief. Offenders could be charged under Rule 14 of the First Schedule Parks Regulation Act, 1872, which insisted that 'no person shall commit any act in violation of Public Decency', but the mere fact that couples were seen lying side by side was not sufficient evidence for police to make an arrest. Dealing with such a matter without corroboration from a second witness required 'extreme tact, a correct demeanour, and knowledge of Police Court ways', according to a memorandum from 1917, and risked accusations of blackmail.

Various attempts to stunt the 'vice' taking place in the park included the production of a notice that was fixed to the entrance gates warning park-goers that 'persons of opposite sexes seen lying on the grass together in violation of public decency are liable to be charged'. Other suggestions considered by police included reinstating plain-clothes police officers; closing the park at 11pm; and increasing the number of officers

on patrol. 'Even with 50 men at my disposal,' wrote Inspector Plume, 'I could not undertake to prevent it altogether … It is only by lighting, and more lighting, that you will ever change the character of Hyde Park.' Unfortunately, his preferred preventative approach of installing lights across the whole of Hyde Park – as opposed to just sections of it, which would 'only have the effect of driving these people elsewhere' – was not within Plume's reach, and he was forced into dealing instead with 'the offensive litter left behind' – as illustrated in the plan pictured here, with the areas considered by Plume to be most troublesome flagged in red.

Map of areas of immorality in Hyde Park, 1937.

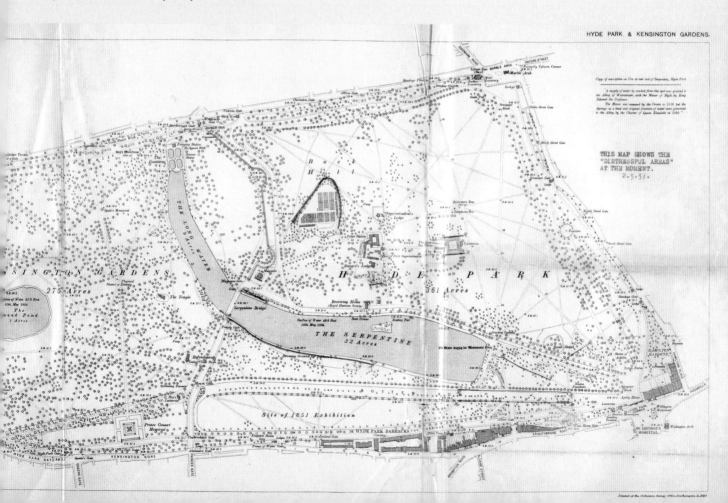

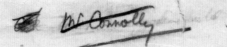

Telephone: TEMPLE BAR 1483.

LONDON PUBLIC MORALITY COUNCIL

President and Chairman

THE LORD BISHOP OF LONDON.

Deputy Chairman
ARCHIBALD J. ALLEN, ESQ.

Vice-Chairmen:
REV. THOMAS NIGHTINGALE.
MRS. JAMES GOW.
ARTHUR R. MORO, ESQ.
REV. A. BINKS.
MISS EDITH NEVILLE

Joint Hon. Treasurers:
EARL OF DYSART AND
LORD KINNAIRD.

Solicitor:
CHALTON HUBBARD, ESQ., J.P.

Bankers:
MESSRS. BARCLAY'S BANK, LTD.
1, PALL MALL EAST, S.W.

Auditors:
MESSRS. HILL, VELLACOTT & CO.

VICE-PRESIDENTS:

LORD BISHOP OF SOUTHWARK.
RT. REV. BISHOP TALBOT.
RT. REV. BISHOP TAYLOR-SMITH.
RT. REV. BISHOP OF KENSINGTON.
RT. REV. BISHOP OF KINGSTON.
RT. REV. BISHOP OF STEPNEY.
RT. REV. BISHOP OF WILLESDEN.
BISHOP PERRIN
VEN. ARCHDEACON OF LONDON.
THE REV. PREBENDARY CARLILE
REV. DR. GILLIE.
THE REV. DR. SCOTT LIDGETT.
REV. HENRY CARTER.
GENERAL HIGGINS (Salvation Army)
THE HON. MRS. E. S. TALBOT.
MRS. BRAMWELL BOOTH.
MRS HUGH PRICE HUGHES
LIEUT.-GENERAL SIR A. E. CODRINGTON,
K.C.B.
SIR FRANCIS CHAMPNEYS, BT.
DR. B. M. ALLEN.
MR. CLAUDE G. MONTEFIORE.
MR. HARRY LLOYD.
MR. CECIL POLHILL.
MR. E. SMALLWOOD.
MR. C. H. WAINWRIGHT, J.P.
MR. HERBERT WARD (representing Cardinal
Archbishop of Westminster).
RT. HON. LORD DICKINSON, G.B.E.
REV. DAWNAY SWINNY.

EXECUTIVE COMMITTEE:

*The President, Deputy Chairman and
Vice-Chairmen.*
MISS BAGGALLAY.
MRS. PERCY BIGLAND.
COMMISSIONER MISS COX, C.B.E.
MR. ROBERTS CRICHTON
THE LADY BERTHA DAWKINS.
MISS DUGDALE.
MRS. DURELL.
MISS GOWERS.
MR. CLARENCE HOOPER.
MRS. HORNIBROOK.
REV. G. KENDALL, O.B.E.
MR. A. B. KENT.
MRS. MAUDE.
MISS MacDOUGALL.
REV. CANON MAPLESDEN.
REV. CLARENCE MAY.
MISS MYLNE
MARJORIE, THE LADY NUNBURNHOLME.
MRS. EDWIN ORDE.
HON. ELEANOR PLUMER.
REV. C. E. SECCOMBE.
MR. F. SEMPKINS.
REV. E. E. SEYZINGER.
REV. P. W. SHEPHERD SMITH.
REV. W. SOUTH.
MR. ASHLEY STABLES.
SISTER THORPE.
MR. E. B. TURNER.
MISS TURNER.
REV. H. COXWELL WHITE.

Secretary:
MR. HOWARD M. TYRER.

37, NORFOLK STREET,
STRAND, W.C.2

11th March, 1931.

Rt. Hon. G. Lansbury M.P.
First Commissioner of Works,
Office of Works,
Whitehall, S.W.1.

Sir,

RE CONDUCT IN HYDE PARK.

I was instructed by the Council at their last
meeting to write to you expressing their deep concern
at the prevalence of improper and indecent conduct in the
open spaces of the Park during the summer of 1930
and the fact that in the latter months of the year, the
number of convictions arose to over 100 persons.

They recognise and appreciate the efforts of the
Police to remedy the abuses complained of, but would
respectfully urge that for the prevention of such
occurences in 1931, early steps be taken to increase
the number of uniformed male and female Police Officers
patrolling the Park and that special supervision of
the parts open to abuse be undertaken.

I beg to remain,
Yours obedient servant,

Howard M. Tyre

Secretary.

14. May 1931.

Dear Sir.

Our Society being very much in sympathy with the work which is being done by the London Public Morality Council, in desiring to secure greater vigilance in control of conditions in Hyde Park. I beg to enclose Resolution with which we are in favour, and Memorial signed by the Officers of our Society.

Yours truly

Kathleen M. A. Wilkinson
(Miss K. Wilkinson)   Hon. Secretary.

To the First Commissioner of Works
     Storeys Gate
                        S.W.

---

14 May 1931

Dear Sir

    Our Society being very much in sympathy
with the work which is being done by the London
Public Morality Council, in desiring to secure
greater vigilance in control of conditions in
Hyde Park. I beg to enclose resolution with
which we are in favour and memorial signed by
the officers of our Society.

        Kathleen M. A. Wilkinson

            Hon. Secretary

To the First Commissioner of Works

Storeys Gate

Devotion or delusion?

The Kray twins' father writes in support of his sons

4 NOVEMBER 1956

In 1956, the twenty-three-year-old Reggie and Ronnie Kray were yet to commit their most heinous crimes, but they were still no angels...

By the age of sixteen the twins had their own gang in the East End, were training as boxers, and were already notorious for causing trouble and getting into fights – often with an arsenal of weapons at hand.

A case against them for causing grievous and actual bodily harm to rivals outside a dance hall in Hackney was heard at the Old Bailey in 1950, but the pair were acquitted due to a lack of evidence. A year later, both boys were charged with assaulting a police officer, but only received probation.

At eighteen years of age Reggie and Ronnie were called up for National Service with the Royal Fusiliers, but on reporting for duty they decided to leave immediately. An officer tried to stop the boys, and received a punch to the chin from Ronnie that left him seriously injured. The twins walked home but were arrested and sent back to the army the next morning. Their service was notable for its violence and repeated attempts to desert. On one occasion of absence without leave they assaulted a police officer and were sent to prison. After more bad behaviour in prison, including assaulting guards, stealing and arson, they both received dishonourable discharges from the army.

However, it was in 1956, during a trial for grievous bodily harm and for Ronnie carrying a loaded revolver, that the Kray twins' father – Charles Snr – was prompted to write this letter.

Reggie and Ronnie, along with two of their gang, Robert Ramsey and William Jones, had seriously assaulted a man called Terence Martin outside their billiards hall in Stepney and put him in hospital.

Ramsey and Jones confessed and pleaded guilty, and were sentenced to imprisonment. Reggie pleaded not guilty due to not being with the others during the assault, and was acquitted. Ronnie, having originally denied the charges, confessed and was sentenced to two years' imprisonment.

Charles Kray states in his letter to the courts that he is convinced Ronnie did not intend to commit violence in the brawl, and that the twins were 'the most respectful and goodnatured lads anybody could wish to meet' – a fairly outlandish notion given their history of violence. The twins were famed for their love, respect and good treatment of their mother, but it seems rather far-fetched to think that this was extended to many others. Charles's letter shows his real concern to be the separation of the twins while Ronnie would be in prison, and how they would be affected. Perhaps this worry foreshadowed the mental health issues suffered by Ronnie, who was soon to be diagnosed with paranoid schizophrenia.

A father's plea for leniency and promises of reform in the bosom of the family are understandable, but the letter does suggest that Charles Kray may have wilfully disregarded the twins' reputation and prior offences in his assessment of them as wanting to 'lead moral and good lives'. Perhaps things may have turned out differently for the infamous Kray brothers if this appeal had been given more consideration, but the die seemed to have been cast for Ronnie and Reggie by this point.

Reggie and Ronnie Kray at home in London after spending 36 hours helping the police with enquiries about the murder of George Cornell, in 1966.

W. C. Kray
Le Kray Nov 14   178 Valance Rd
Bethnal Green
E.2.

Dear Sir/

May I respectfully
submit this appeal to you from
a father, pleading for his Son.
It is my firm belief that he
was intimidated in this brawl
more out of curiosity than any
intentions of committing any violence
of which he was innocent I am
fully convinced, If you will
at least believe me sir they
are the most respectful + good
natured lads anybody could
wish to meet so kind to
my Wife + I + everybody
in their thoughts + actions + only

willing to help anybody. So
could you realize as I, that
the separating of these Boys
could be a vast setback in the
future of their young lives. so
I appeal to you Sir with
your kindness & far reaching
thoughts & vast experience If
you will only deal with him
as lenient as you possibly
can, he would compensate your
leniency by remaining a good
citizen as ever. Nobody
could wish for a more
kindly lad or his brother, to
my wife & I & everybody
all their concern in life is to

3/

do good to everybody & with
my guidance & my Wife, Son
Charles (the eldest Brother) they
will make good. (4) once again
I appeal to you for my sake &
his mothers, assuring you it
could be a great influence over
both the boians way of life
They are at present in a good
business with every chance of
making good. but I appeal
to you again for a chance
to enable this lad of mine
to lead a moral & good
life. Hoping my appeal may
receive your kind consideration &
mercy
                    I am Sir
            Yours Faithfully
               Mr. C Kray

```
                        Mr C Kray
Sunday Nov 4th          178 Valance Rd
                        Bethnal Green
                                    E2
```

Dear Sir

     May I respectfully submit this appeal
to you from a father, pleading for his Son.
It is my firm belief that he was intimidated
in this brawl more out of curiosity than any
intentions of committing any violence of which
he was innocent I am fully convinced. If you
will at least believe me that they are the most
respectful and good natured lads anybody could
wish to meet, so kind to my Wife & I & everybody
in their thoughts & actions & only willing to
help anybody. Sir, could you realise as I, that
the separating of these Boys could be a vast
setback in the future of their young lives. So
I appeal to you Sir, with your kindness and far
reaching thoughts & vast experience if you will
only deal with him as lenient as you possibly
can, he would compensate your leniency by
remaining a good citizen as ever. Nobody could
wish for a more kindly lad & his brother, to my
wife and I & everybody all their concern in life
is to do good to everybody & with my guidance &
my Wife & Son Charles (the eldest Brother) they
will make good. Sir, once again I appeal to you
for my sake & his mother's, assuring you it could
be a great influence over both the Twins way of
life. They are at present in a good business with
every chance of making good. Can I appeal to you
again for a chance to enable this lad of mine to
lead a moral and good life. Hoping my appeal may
receive your kind consideration & mercy.

I am, Sir
Yours Faithfully
Mr C Kray

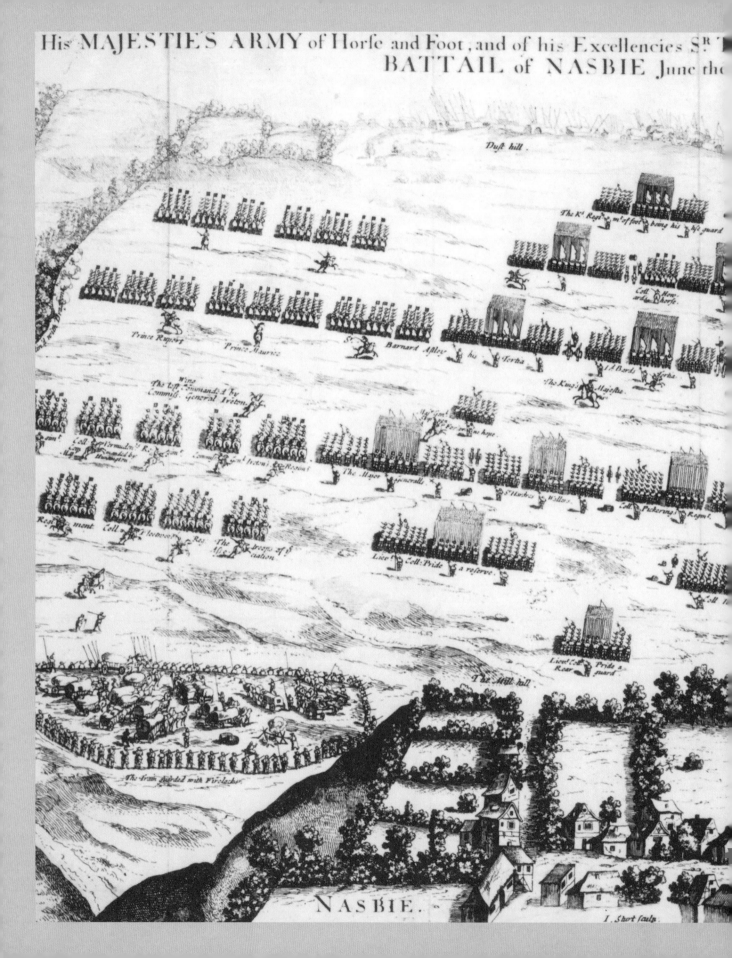

MAS FAIREFAX : as they were drawn into feveral l
1645.

Politics and power

A subtext of murder?

King John to his advisors and his mother, Eleanor of Aquitaine

16 APRIL 1203

To a modern reader, this does not look much like a letter at all. The original letter was sent by King John, who was in Normandy, to his advisors, including his mother, Eleanor of Aquitaine, in England. When the letter arrived at court a copy of it was written on to a large roll, kept for just this purpose. It is this roll, along with thousands of others like it, that survives at The National Archives, providing an amazing record of the correspondence sent out by medieval kings and their closest advisors. This letter is in effect the file copy.

It does not seem very dramatic at first glance. King John is at his castle of Falaise in Normandy, and he writes to his leading advisors telling them that everything is fine and that they should have faith in what his messenger, Brother John de Valerant, tells them. The letter is brief and businesslike, but there is a great deal more to it than meets the eye.

John had succeeded his older brother, Richard I, as King of England and Duke of Normandy in 1199. However, his succession was not uncontested: John and Richard had a nephew, Arthur, the son of their late brother Geoffrey, Duke of Brittany. Under the fluid medieval rules of succession, many people backed Arthur's claim to the English throne, including John's arch-enemy, King Philip of France.

Philip took advantage of the confusion following Richard I's death to invade John's duchy of Normandy, in alliance with Arthur, leading to several years of intermittent fighting in France. In April 1202, John's forces surprised Arthur at Mirebeau and captured him and many of his leading supporters. Arthur's sister, Eleanor, was dispatched to England, but Arthur was taken as a captive to John's stronghold at Falaise. A year later, he was moved to another castle at Rouen. After this, Arthur, still only fifteen years old, was never seen in public again.

Exactly what happened to the teenager has been the cause of much debate. One chronicler wrote that on Maundy Thursday (3 April) 1203, John flew into a rage and struck Arthur with a rock, killing him. Another told that while still at Falaise John had pleaded with his nephew to abandon his alliance with Philip of France and adhere to John's side, but Arthur had haughtily refused. Thus John decided that he needed to

King John.

permanently remove this thorn from his side, and sent him to Rouen to be killed. While more calculated, this theory of events is also more unsettling.

The letter here was written by John within a couple of weeks of Arthur's presumed death. So, when John wrote that matters in Normandy were going very well, is it possible that he was referring to the murder of his own brother's son? He could not, of course, commit this thought to writing, but he could rely on his messenger to impart the news. We should recall, too, that one of the recipients of the letter was John's mother, the dowager queen Eleanor of Aquitaine. She was a staunch supporter of John – but nonetheless, her son was responsible for the death of her grandson.

With this context in mind, John's brief letter becomes a chilling and unnerving read.

Eleanor of Aquitaine. The drawing is taken from the carving on her tomb at Fontevrault.

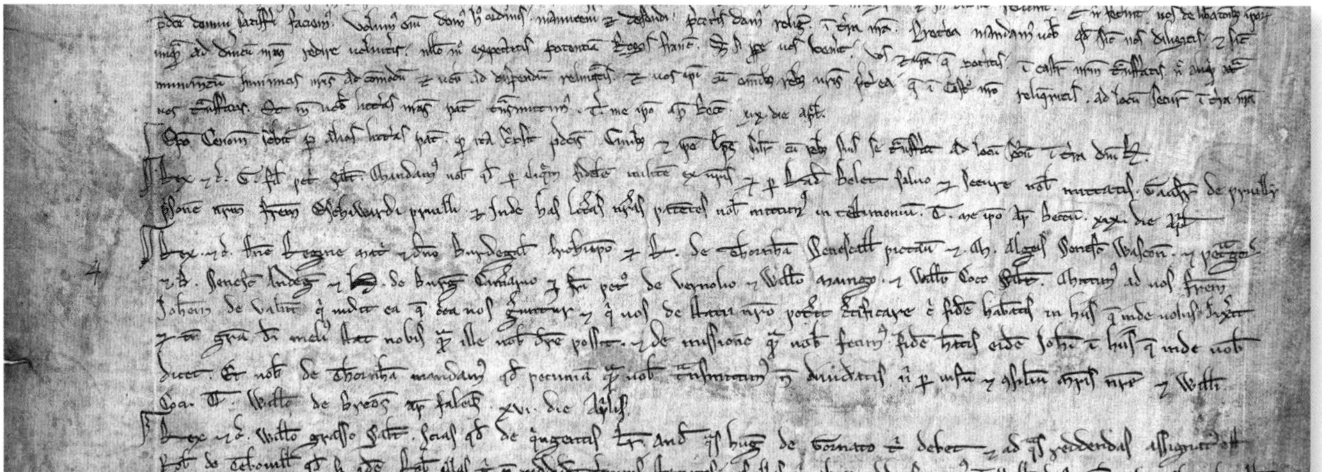

King John to his mother, Queen Eleanor of Aquitaine, and others

The King etc to the Lady Queen his mother, and the Lord Archbishop of Bordeaux, and Richard of Thornham seneschal of Poitou, and Martin Algais seneschal of Gascony and Perigord, and Bricius seneschal of Anjou, and Hubert de Burgh Chamberlain, and Brother Peter de Vernol, and William Maingo, and William Cocus, greetings.

We send to you Brother John de Valerant who has seen those things which are progressing with regard to us and who will be able to inform you about our situation. You should have faith in him in respect of those things which he will tell to you. Nevertheless the grace of God is even more with us than he can tell you; and concerning the mission which we have made to you, you should have faith in those things which the same John will tell you. And we command you, Richard of Thornham, not to distribute the money that we have transmitted to you, unless through the sight and counsel of our mother and William Cocus. Witness William de Briouze at Falais, on the 16th day of April.

Seeking the seal of approval
Letter from Richard III to his chancellor, Bishop John Russell

12 OCTOBER 1483

In this letter from 12 October 1483, King Richard III shows just how involved medieval kings were in running government and in managing political events as they unfolded.

When the letter was written, King Richard was at Lincoln awaiting news of a landing by the forces of the exiled Henry Tudor, Earl of Richmond (later King Henry VII), who was sailing from Brittany. While there, Richard learned that Henry Stafford, 2nd Duke of Buckingham (one of Richard's key allies in his grab for the throne four months earlier), had also joined the rebellion. Few doubted that Buckingham's own claim to the throne would stay sidelined if the uprising gained momentum.

The letter reveals that Richard is most concerned that he does not have the Great Seal of England with him; use of the seal on official documents was the most solemn and comprehensive way of asserting the King's wishes. The chancellor (the officer in charge of government administration), John Russell, Bishop of Lincoln, had been ill and was unable to travel northwards with the King. Without possession of the seal, Richard could not be certain that all aspects of government were under his control; if the seal were to fall into the hands of his enemies or rebels then they could issue orders, instructions or grants that would undermine or confuse Richard's leadership. The King evidently felt that the formal command by warrant – written by one of his clerks – was not powerful enough to convey his royal frustration. He therefore wrote in his own hand – a very rare instance on official warrants – a further, more personal message to Bishop Russell: if he is unable to travel with the seal in person, then he is to send a trusted man with it as soon as possible.

The great seal of Richard III that was so crucial for validating the king's orders and correspondence.

Richard also announces that his preparations have gone well and he is ready to fight for his crown, but his anger at the defection of Buckingham is clear. The duke is described as 'the most untrue creature living', a reference to the gifts of land and power that Richard had already granted to his former ally. More of Richard's thinking about the malicious and ungrateful duke would be passed on by word of mouth by the bearer of the message, one of the King's heralds.

This letter merges the official and personal aspects of a king's role in the late medieval period. Royal leaders were expected to show in their demeanour, words and actions those qualities that made them fit to rule. Richard III here offers a glimpse into the thought processes and concerns of a king who had just realised that unfolding events were putting his authority at risk. His instant response to the latest news, typified by his scrawled message to his chancellor, only confirms how precarious was the grip on power during times of civil war and rebellion.

Weeks of storms and flooding prevented Tudor's forces from landing in time. Buckingham, meanwhile, was trapped by the swollen rivers in the Marches of Wales. He was betrayed by a servant and beheaded at Salisbury on 2 November before getting a chance to plead with the King. Tudor tried again in August 1485, this time having more success in gaining enough support to challenge King Richard on the battlefield. His amazing victory at the Battle of Bosworth on 22 August 1485 ushered in the start of the Tudor dynasty.

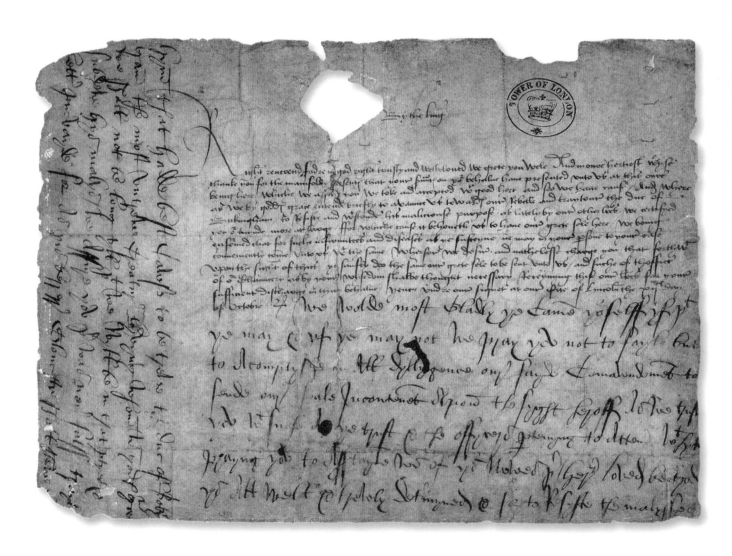

Right reverend father in God, right trusty and welbeloved we greet you well. And in our heartiest wise thank you for the manifold presents that your servants on your behalf have presented unto us at that our being here, which we assure you we took and accepted with good heart, and so we have cause. And whereas we by God's grace intend briefly to advance us towards our rebel and traitor the duke of Buckingham to resist and withstand his malicious purpose as lately by our letters we certified you (of) our mind more at large. For which cause it behoves us to have our great seal here. We being informed that for certain infirmities and diseases as you sustain you may not in your person to your ease conveniently come unto us with the same. Wherefore we desire and nevertheless charge you that forthwith upon the sight of these you safely do the same our great seal to be sent unto us, and such of the officers of our Chancery as by your wisdom shall be thought necessary. Receiving these our letters for your sufficient discharge in that behalf. Given under our signet at our city of Lincoln, the 12th day of October.

We would most gladly you came yourself if that you may, and if you may not we pray you not to fail but to accomplish in all diligence our said commandment to send our seal incontinent upon the sight hereof as we trust you with such as we trust, and the officers pertaining to attend with it, praying you to ascertain us of your news. Here, loved be God, is all well and truly determined and for to resist the duke of Buckingham the most untrue creature living, whom with God's grace we shall not be long until that we will be in that [sic] parts and subdue his malice. We assure you that never was false traitor better provided for as this bearer, Gloucester, can show.

A ribald recommendation
The Duke of Norfolk to Thomas Cromwell, Lord Privy Seal

5 JUNE 1537

Written at Sheriff Hutton in Yorkshire a few months after the popular rising known as the Pilgrimage of Grace and during the early stages of the dissolution of the monasteries, the Duke of Norfolk's letter opens with a reference to the gold and silver riches seized for King Henry VIII from the priory of Bridlington. The property of the priory was forfeit to the Crown after its prior, William Wood, had been executed earlier in 1537 for his role in the rebellion.

The bearer of this letter and the gold ornaments, one Tristram Teshe, was at this point a receiver for the Archbishop of York. He had presumably suffered the loss of goods at the hands of the rebels, as Norfolk solicits Cromwell's favour in the light of his misfortune. However, Norfolk's attitude is not wholly charitable as he goes on to suggest that Cromwell may wish to flirt with Teshe's wife or maidservant when staying in his house in York – 'if ye Lust not to daly with his wif[e], he hath a yowng woman with praty proper tetins'.

Thomas Cromwell.

Norfolk then asks for a further favour from Cromwell, who has previously ordered St Mary's Abbey in York to relinquish part of their property to a particular individual. The duke is persuaded by the abbot's argument that this would impact on the abbey's ability to offer hospitality and questions whether one man should profit at the expense of many people's livelihoods.

The letter concludes with a paragraph in Norfolk's own handwriting (the main body of the letter being written by a scribe), which reads as a slightly irritable afterthought, suggesting the King is wasting his money keeping a garrison at Pontefract (which had temporarily fallen to rebels the previous year).

Norfolk's signature suggests a man of many facets. The jaggedly angular 'T Norfolk' is finished off with a softer flourish depicting a cloverleaf.

This letter provides an intriguing glimpse into the relationship between these two men, who are sometimes depicted as being antagonistic because of their class differences but were clearly sufficiently comfortable with one another to communicate about personal as well as state matters.

Lord Thomas Howard, Duke of Norfolk.

My verey good Lorde with most herty recommendac[i]ons
This shalbe to advertise you that by Tristram Teshe
the berer I do nowe sende to the kinges highnes in twoo
boxes all suche golde stuffe as was uppon the shryne
at bridlyngton, and with the same one lre to his ma[ges]tie
to knowe his pleasure what shalbe done with
the rest of tyme, as by the saide lre yo[ur] good
Lordshipp shall p[er]ceyve   35

My Lord I require you to be good lorde unto the
saide Teshe, assuryng you I pitie hym most
of any man that hath be spoyled, for farr oftyn
or at thes[e] howre withowt restitucion or
agrement made with them, And unto hym I say not
for the manyes howe it shalbe possible to brynge
hym to so moche of his goodes, but that he shall
largely susteyne, by cause that he may not yet
knowe his spoylers, and in his case truly,
doth remayne, eftsones requiryng you to be his good
lorde, and to be content to lodge in his house
at yo[ur] comyng to yorke, thoughe the house be not
great, it is of the best sorte of that order and
verey nere to the kinges lodgyng, And ye may be
sure to be wellcome, And if ye lust not to dale
with his wife, he hath a younge woman with
praty proper gitens/

Also I require you to be good lorde to thabbot of
S[ein]te Mary Abbay, who hath of late receyved a lre
from you in the favo[u]r of ffalkon, for a ferme
assuryng your good lordeshippe that the saide ferme
is so necessary for the saide abbay that withowt
the same it is not possible to contynewe theyr
hospitalite as they doo, for and they sholde
foo withowt it, they sholde be inforced to bye the
provisions in the market, And pitie it were that
for one mans oughte, so many p[er]sons sholde wante
theyr lyvynge/ I am sory I have so moche to trowble
you to you in my lres, consyderyng his ill p[er]donage
in this matier And thus the holy trenite sende yow
thaccomplishment of yo[ur] gentle hertt desyres, ffrom
Ghertshey the viij day of June.

Also my lord I understande the kinge doth kepe a
garyson at pomfret which in myn opinion is
money spent about nede
                                    yo[ur] assured

My veray good Lorde with most herty rec[c]omendac[i]ons
Thies shalbe tadvertise youe that by Tristram Tashe
this berer I do nowe sende to the kinges highnes in twoo
boxes all suche gold Stuff as was uppon the Shryne
at brydlyngton, and with the same one L[ette]re to his ma
iestie to knowe his pleasure what shalbe done w[i]th
the rest of Sylver as by the saide l[ette]re yo[ur] good
Lordshippe shall p[er]ceyve

My Lord I require youe to be good lord unto the
saide Tashe, assuryng youe I pitie hym most
of any man that hath be spoyled, for fewe others
ar at this howre withowt restituc[i]on, or
agreme[n]t made with them. And unto hym I can not
see the meanys howe it shalbe possible to bryng
hym to so moche of his gooddes, but that he shall
largely susteyne, by cause that he can not p[ro]ve
who were his spoylers, and in this cace he only
doth remayne, eftsones requiring youe to be his
good Lorde And to be content to lodge in his howse
at yo[ur] cu[m]myng to yo[r]ke, thought the house be
not great, it is of the best sorte of that Citie and
veray nere to the kinges lodgyng, and ye may be
sure to be welcome, And if ye Lust not to daly
with his wif, he hath a yowng woman with
praty proper tetins

Also I require youe to be good Lorde to Thabbot of
Saincte Mary Abbay, who hath of Late receyved a l[ette]re
from youe in the favo[ur] of Fulbery for a Ferme
assuryng your good lordeshippe that the said Ferme
is so necessary for the saide abbay that withowte
the same it is not possible to contynewe their
hospitalitie as they doo, for and they shold
goo withowte it, they shold be inforced to bye ther
p[ro]visions in the Market. And pitie it were that
for one Mans p[ro]fight, So many p[er]sones shold want
ther lyvinges. I am sory I have so moche reco[m]mended
hym to you in my l[ette]res, consideryng his ill p[ro]cedinges
in this Matier. And thus the holy trinitie send ye
thaccomplissheme[n]t of yo[u]r gentle herts desyres. From
Shrifhoten [Sheriff Hutton] the vth Day of June.

[In Norfolk's hand] also my lord I understande the king doth kepe a
a garyson at pomfret [Pontefract] wiche In myn opinion is
money spent w[i]t[h]out nede

                    yo[ur]s assewredly
                    T Norfolk

                                        Endorsed

                                        To my veray good Lorde
                                        my Lorde pryvey Seale

A royal invitation
Letter to the Prince of Orange inviting him to become England's king

30 JUNE 1688

Seven notable individuals (the so-called Immortal Seven) put their names to a formal letter of invitation to William of Orange, requesting that he make the necessary preparations to depose his father-in-law, James II.

Dissatisfaction with James grew during his short reign (1685–1688), as a result of his attempts to establish a standing army and to introduce religious tolerance, both of which were seen as a prelude to the re-imposition of Catholicism to Britain. As a result, there had been a number of contacts made between James's opponents within Britain and William and his wife, Mary, the eldest of James's daughters (by his first marriage to Anne Hyde).

Although William was more than happy to accept this offer, he was minded to simply wait until James II died; since James had no sons, the succession would pass to Mary. All this changed, however, when Mary of Modena, James's second wife, gave birth to a boy (the future 'Young Pretender'), which ushered in the prospect of a succession of Catholic monarchs. William thus wanted to ensure that there was widespread support for his attempt on the throne (unlike the Duke of Monmouth's disastrous enterprise of 1685) so that he would appear as a liberator rather than a conqueror, and he refused to come unless formally invited.

While none of the Immortal Seven were foolish enough to sign their names on the letter itself, they identified themselves by a secret two digit number code. Both Henry Sidney (thirty-three), who had drafted the invite, and Edward Russell (thirty-five) were leading members of the Whig party, while Henry Compton, Bishop of London (thirty-one) and the Earl of Danby (twenty-seven) were both prominent Tories. Together, these represented a broad selection of the highest level of English society, sufficient to convince William that he would enjoy a suitably wide degree of support from across the country; a country, moreover, that feared a return to the upheaval of civil war.

In their letter, an extract of which is shown here, the seven assured William that 'the people were so generally dissatisfied with the present conduct of the government in relation to their religion, liberties and properties'. They were also at pains to convince William that James and his supporters would be unable to organise any effective opposition 'as we believe their army would be very much divided and that neither could they rely upon the navy as amongst the seamen it is certain that there is not one in ten who would do any service in such a war'. Ironically, it was Rear Admiral Herbert, disguised as a common sailor, who secretly carried the invitation to William at The Hague, and was discreetly referred to as Mr 'H' within its text.

When the Prince landed at Torbay in November 1688 there was no organised resistance, as military support for James rapidly evaporated upon Salisbury Plain. Key royalists such as Major-General John Churchill (a former page to the King) defected to the Williamite side, while English Jacobites either fled to France or formally disappeared from view. The Glorious Revolution therefore became an entirely bloodless coup.

A 1692 portrait of William III of Orange.

June y 30th 1688

224

Wee have great satisfaction to find
by 35, and since by Mons. Fukestem, that
your Hi. is so ready, and willing to give
us such assistances as they have related
to us. Wee have great reason to
beleeve wee shall be every day in a
worse condition then wee are, and
lesse able to defend our selves, and
therefore wee doe earnestly wish,
wee might be so happy as to find
a remedy before it be too late for
us to contribute to our owne deliverance
but although these be our wishes
yet wee will by no meanes put
your Hi. into any expectations
which may misguide your owne
Councills in this matter, so that
the best advice wee can give, is
to informe your Hi. truly, both
of the state of things here at this

and will take care to bring some good
Engeneers with you, and we have
desired Mr H. to consult you about
all such matters, to whom we have
communicated our thoughts, in
many perticulars to bedious, to have
been written, and about which
no certain resolutions can be
taken, till wee have heard again
from your Highnesse.

25. 24. 27. 29. 31. 35. 53.

St: Dr: Jony Linny Holland Ruf: Sidney

June the 30th 1688

We have great satisfaction to find by 35, and since by M. Zulestein, that your Highness is so ready and willing to give us such assistances as they have related to us. We have great reason to believe that we shall be every day in a worse condition than we are and less able to defend ourselves, and therefore we do earnestly wish we might be so happy as to find a remedy before it be too late for us to contribute to our own deliverance; but although these be our wishes yet we will by no means put your Highness into any expectations which may misguide your own counsels in this matter, so that the best advice we can give is to inform your Highness truly both of the state of things here at this time and of the difficulties which appear to us. As to the first, the people are so generally dissatisfied with the present conduct of the Government in relation to their religion, liberties, and properties (all which have been greatly invaded), and they are in such expectation of their prospects being daily worse that your Highness may be assured there are nineteen parts of twenty of the people throughout the Kingdom who are desirous of a change; and who, we believe, would willingly contribute to it if they had such a protection to countenance their rising as could secure them from being destroyed before they could get to be in a posture able to defend themselves. It is no less certain that much the greatest part of the nobility and gentry are as much dissatisfied, although it be not safe to speak to many of them beforehand; and there is no doubt but that some of the most considerable of them would venture themselves with your Highness at first landing, whose interests would be able to draw great numbers to them wherever they could protect the raising and drawing men together. And if such a strength could be landed as were able to defend itself and them, till they could be got together into some order, we make no question but that strength would quickly be increased to a number double to the Army here, although their Army should all remain firm to them. Whereas we do upon very good grounds believe that their Army would then be very much divided among themselves, many of the officers being so discontented that they continue in their service only for a subsistence (besides that, some of their minds are known already) and very many of the common soldiers do daily show such an aversion to the Popish religion that there is the greatest probability imaginable of great numbers of deserters, which would come from them should there be such an occasion; and amongst the seamen it is almost certain there is not one in ten who would do them any service in such a war. Besides all this, we do much doubt whether this present state of things will not yet be much changed to the worse before another year by a great alteration, which will probably be made both in the officers and soldiers of the Army, and by such other changes as are not only to be expected from a packed Parliament, but what the meeting of any Parliament (in our present circumstances) may produce against those, who will be looked upon as principal obstructors of their proceedings there; it being taken for granted that if things cannot then be carried to their wishes in a parliamentary way, other measures will be put in execution by more violent means; and although such proceedings will then heighten the discontents, yet such courses will probably be taken at that time as will prevent all possible means of relieving ourselves.

These considerations make us of opinion that this is a season in which we may more probably contribute to our own safeties than hereafter (although we must own to your Highness there are some judgements differing from ours in this particular) insomuch that, if the circumstances stand so with your Highness that you believe you can yet be time enough in a condition to give assistance this year, sufficient for a relief under these circumstances which have been now represented, we who subscribe this will not fail to attend your Highness upon your landing, and to do all that lies in our power to prepare others to be in as much readiness as such an action is capable of, where there is so much danger in communicating an affair of such a nature, till it be near the time of its being made public. But as we have already told your Highness we must also lay our difficulties before your Highness which are chiefly: that we know not what alarum your preparations for this expedition may give or what notice it will be necessary for you to give the States beforehand, by either of which means their intelligence or suspicions here may be such as may cause us to be secured before your landing; and we must presume to inform your Highness that your compliment upon the birth of the child (which not one in a thousand here believes to be the Queen's) hath done you some injury. The false imposing ofthat upon the Princess and the nation, being not only an infinite exasperation of people's minds here, but being certainly one of the chief causes upon which the declaration of your entering the Kingdom in a hostile manner must be founded on your part, although many other reasons are to be given on ours. If, upon a due consideration of all these circumstances, your Highness shall think fit to adventure upon the attempt, or, at least, to make such preparations for it as are necessary (which we wish you may), there must be no more time lost in letting us know your resolutions concerning it, and in what time we may depend that all the preparations will be ready, as also whether your Highness does believe the preparations can be so managed as not to give them warning here, both to make them increase their force and to secure those they shall suspect would join with you. We need not say anything about ammunitions, artillery, mortar-pieces, spare arms etc., because if you think fit to put anything in execution you will provide enough of these kinds and will take care to bring some good engineers with you; and we have desired Mr. H. to consult you about all such matters, to whom we have communicated our thoughts in many particulars too tedious to have been written, and about which no certain resolutions can be taken, till we have heard again from your Highness.

25; 24; 27; 29; 31; 35; 33.

Stuart diplomacy or veiled criticism?
Charles Edward Stuart to his father, James Edward Stuart

10 SEPTEMBER 1745

'… I keep my health better in these wild mountains than I used to do, in the Campagnie Felice [happy company], and sleep sounder lying on the ground than I used to do in the palaces at Rome.'

In this description, Charles Edward Stuart paints a wholesome and humble portrait of his experiences leading the 1745 Jacobite risings, one that goes some way to constructing the romantic image of the 'Bonnie Prince Charlie' that is still so familiar in the popular imagination. The rising ultimately failed, but in the early heady days of the invasion the momentum was with the Jacobites, and this letter sought to tap into the energy and popular support for the Stuart cause.

Addressing his father, James Edward Stuart, who had led a failed invasion in 1715, Charles writes that 'since my landing everything has succeeded to meet my wishes' and that he has an army of 'brave and determined men who are resolved to die or conquer with me'. He emphasises the Stuart unity of the cause by stating that he has followed his father's advice to rule with 'justice and clemency' and that as a result he has won their 'hearts' and 'to see the love and harmony that reigns amongst us, he would be apt to look upon it as a large well-ordered family in which everyone loves another better than himself'. Charles constructs an image of a fair, kind ruler, and one who has the full support of his army.

However, as the letter goes on the promotion of the Jacobite cause begins to seem a little too perfect. Charles comprehensively addresses the concerns of those opposing the return to Stuart rule, declaring that 'for all that while I breathe I will never consent to alienate one foot of land that belongs to the Crown of England, or set my hand to any treaty inconsistent with its independency and sovereignty'. The letter continues to become a platform for explaining past errors, and he refers to his 'grandfather's unhappy reign' and how 'unreasonable' it would be to suppose that 'your Majesty, who is so sensible of, and has so often considered the fatal errors of your father, would with your eyes open go and repeat them again?' To temper the fears of foreign invasion he is careful to note that if French troops were to invade they 'should come only as friends to assist your majesty in the recovery of your just right, the weak people would believe

Charles Edward Stuart, 'Bonnie Prince Charlie'.

they came as invaders'. Furthermore, to counter anxiety over the imposition of
Catholicism, Charles writes with perhaps false sincerity, 'I must not close this letter
without doing justice to your Majesty's Protestant subjects, who I find are as fully
as zealous in your cause as the Roman Catholics'.

What are we to make of this politic letter that masquerades as one from a loyal son
to his wise father? The historian Jacqueline Riding has suggested that 'the letter is so
balanced, fair-minded, even magnanimous and frankly better spelt than Charles' usual
letters … that one can imagine it was written with the aid of another and with a much
broader audience in mind than his father'. She also notes that all was not as well in
the Jacobite camp as he suggested.

The fact that we hold a copy of the letter and not the original, and that it is found
in the papers of the Secretary of State for Scotland, indicates that the letter was
forwarded to government officials. Indeed, it seems that it was in the hand of Lord
President Duncan Forbes, who was actively sending intelligence about the Jacobites
to the Hanoverian government. Historians usually refer to a printed copy of the letter,
and the presence of minor differences between the printed version and the one The
National Archives holds suggests that there may have been multiple copies of letters
in circulation. By revisiting the archival context of the letter we are able to grasp the
more complex motivations behind it, and to see how the Jacobites harnessed the
culture of letter-writing and circulation to argue their cause.

If I make one hospital of a Church, it would be looked upon as a great profanation, and if I make...
mens Loafs for that people, I shall be accused by my ungenerous enemys of having violated my Manifesto, in which...
... to violate no mans property, if the magistrates would act, they could help me out of this difficulty, come what will...
I am resolved I won't suffer the poor wounded men to lye in the Streets, and if I can doe no better, I will make a hospital
of the Palace and leave it to them I am so much distracted with these cares, joyn with those of my own people,
that I have only time to add that I am Your M: M D : S : B O : S : C.

97

Perth Sept. 10 1745

Since my Landing every thing has succeeded to me to my wishes, it has pleased god to prosper me hitherto even beyond my expec-
-tation, I have got together about 2000 (and as promised more) brave determined men, who are resolved to die or conquer with me. The
enemy marched a body of regular troops to attack me, but when they came near they changed their mind by taking a different route
and by making forced marches they have escaped unto the North to the great disappointment of my Highland ones; but I am not at all
sorry for it, I shall have the greater glory by beating them when they grow more dangerous and supported by their Dragoons. I have occa-
-sion to reflect every day upon your Majys last words to me, viz: that I would find power if it was not accompanied with Justice and
Clemency, an uneasy thing to me, I feel and grievous to those unhappy. tis owing to the observance of this rule and my conforming my self to the custom
-ms of those people that I have got their hearts to a degree not to be easily conceived by those who are not here. One who observes the discipline
I have established would take my little army to be a body of pickt veterans, and to see the love and harmony that reigns amongst us, he would
be apt to look upon it as a large, well ordered family in which every one loves another better than himself. I keep my health better
on these wild Mountains than I used to doe in the Campania Felice, and sleep sounder lying on the ground than I used to doe in the Palaces at
Rome. There is one thing, and but one, in which I have had any difference with my faithfull Highlanders; it was about setting a price
upon my Enemys head, which knowing your Majys generous and humane temper sure will shock you as much as it did me when first
I knew the Proclamation setting a price on my head, I would and treated it with disdain it deserved, upon which they flew out into a most
violent rage and insisted on my doing the same by him, as this flowed solely from the poor mens love and concern for me and not knowing
how to be angry with them for it, and try'd to bring them to temper by representing to them that it was a mean barbarous practice among Princes
that must dishonour them in the eyes of all men of honour, that I could not see how my Cousins having set me the example would justifie
me in imitating that which I blame so much in him. But nothing I said would satisfie them, some went even so far as to say, I shall never
and venture our lives for a man who seems so indifferent about preserving his own? I have been drawn into a thing for which I con-
demn my self, Your Majy knowes that in my nature I am neither cruel nor revengefull, and god who knows my heart knows that if the very
Prince who has forced me to this (for tis he that has forced me) was in my power, the greatest pleasure I could feel would be treating
him as the brave black Prince treated his prisoner the King of France, to make him ashamed of having shown himself so inhumane an
enemy to a mon for attempting a thing which he himself... would beg me for not staying time.
I beg your Majy would be under no uneasyness about me, he is safe thats in gods keeping, if soe it shall be, as those lord
will ensue. And the pleasure I take in thinking I have a way in all respects more worthy, by my self to support your
Majys Just cause, and rescue my injured country from the oppression under which it groans, (if it will suffer it self to
be rescued) makes life more indifferent to me, as I know and admire the fortitude with which your Majy has sup-
-ported your Misfortunes, and the generous disdain with which you have constantly rejected all offers of foreign
assistance on terms which you thought dishonourable to your self and my own to your country, if our deluded
interested friends should at this time take advantage of that tender affection with which they know you love
me, I hope you will reject them with the same magnanimity you have hitherto shown, and leave me to trust
myself for my self as Edwd the 3d left his brave son when he, my injured countrys, in danger of being oppressed by nukes in the field
No Sir let it never be said that to save your son you injured your country. When your Enemys being
aided by own Forreigners and you reject all forreign assistance on dishonourable terms, your deluded
subjects of England must see who is the true father of the child. For my own part I declare to the
national one foot of land that belongs to the
Crown of England or set my head to any treaty inconsistant with its independency
and Sovereignty. If the English would have my life let them take it, if they can but no purchase no price
kindness on their part shall ever force me to doe a thing that may give the there so taking
it, I may be overcome by my Enemy, but I won't dishonour my self: if I die, it shall be with my Sword in my hand, fighting for
the liberty of those who fight against me. I know there will be fulsome addresses from the different corporations of
England, but I hope they will employ one none but the lowest and most ignorant of the people. They will try no doubt
to revive all the errors and excesses of my Grandfathers unhappy reign and impute them to your Majy and me who
had no hand in them and suffered most by them. Can any thing be more unreasonable, than to suppose that your
Majy who is so sensible of, and has so often condemned the fatal errors of your father, would with your eyes open
give and repeat them again? Notwithstanding the repeated assurances you Majy has given in your declaration, and
I in my Manifesto, that you will invade no mans property, they endeavour to persuade the unthinking people. Not
one of the first things they are to respect, will be to see the publick credit destroyed as if it would be your in-
-ention to render your self contemptible in the eyes of all the nations of Europe, and all the Kingdoms you promise
to reign over not at home, and insignificant abroad. They no doubt try to hark to frighten the present possessors
of Church and Abby lands with vain terrors as if your Majys intention was to resume them all, not considering
that you have lived too long in Roman Catholick countrys, and read the history of England so carefully, not to have
observed the many Melancholy Monuments to be seen their of the folly of those pious but weak Princes, who
thinking to honour religion have hurt it, by heaping superfluous riches on the Church, whereby they have in reason-
-bly nursed up a power that has too often proved an over match for their Successors.
I find it a great loss the brave Ld Marischall is not with me, his character is very high in
this country, as it must be, wherever he is known, I doe they see him then a 1000 french, who if they would
come only as friends to assist your Majy in the recovery of your just right, the weak people would
believe they came as invaders. There is one man of this country, who I would wish to have my friend,
and that is the D: of Argyle who I hear is in high credit among them on account of his great ability and
good qualities, and has many dependents by his large fortune: but I am told I can hardly flatter my
self with the hopes of it, the hard usage which his family received from our sunk deep in his mind.
What have those princes to answer for who by their cruelty have raised enemies not only to themselves
but their innocent children. I must not close this little without doeing justice to your Majys
protestant subjects, who I find are fully as zealous in your cause as the Roman Catholicks, which
is what honest Dr Wagstaff has often told me I would find when I came to try them. I design to
march from hence to morrow, and I hope my next shall be from Edr from your M: M:
O: S and D: St C

Since my last from Perth it has pleased god to prosper your Matys Armes under... my last... much as has even surpassed my wishes, on the 21st ... Sr John ... and got possession of the town without firing a shot ... the drops of blood or commit the least violence, and this morning I have gained a most signal victory with Little or no loss: If I had a squadron or two of horse to pursue the flying enemy there would not one man of them have escaped, as it is they have hardly saved any but a few dragoons who by a most precipitate flight will I believe get into Berwick. If I...

I obtained this victory over foreigners my joy would been compleat, but as it is over english men it has thrown a damp upon it that I little ... imagined, the men I have defeat were your Matys enemys its true, but they might have become your friends and dutyfull subjects, when they had got their eyes opened to see the true interest of their country which I am come to save and not to destroy; for this reason I have discharged all publick rejoycings. I do not care to enter into the particulars of the action and chuse rather that your Maty should hear it from another then from my self. I send this by Stewart to whome you may give entire credit he is a faithfull honest fellow and thoroughly instructed in everything that has happened to this day. I shall have a loss in him, but I hope it will soon be made up to me by his speedy return with the most agreeable news I can receive. I mean that of your Matys and my dearest brothers health.

I have seen two or three Gazettes filled with Addresses and Mandates from the Bishops to their Clergy, the Addresses one such as I expected and can impose on none but the weak and credulous. The Mandates are of the same sort but more artfully drawn up: they order their clergy to make the people sensible of the great blessings they enjoy under the present family that governs them, particularly of the strict administration of Justice, of the sacred regard thats paid to the laws, and the great security of their religion and property. This sounds all very well, and makes impression on the unthinking, but one who reads with a little care will easily see the fallacy; what occasion has a prince that has learnt the secret of corrupting the fountain of all law and Justice, the Parliament, to give and pull of the Mask by openly violating all the gentle allows and disturbing the ordinary course of Justice? I would not thus be to give the alarme and amount to telling them that he was not come to protect as he pretended but really to betray them. When they talk of the Security of their religion they can not ... mention one word of the dreadfull growth of Atheism and Infidelity which I am credibly sorry to hear from very sensible men will... in these few years is gone to a flaming height, even so far that I am assured many of their most fashionable men one ashamed to own themselves Xtians, and many of the lower sort act as if they were not. Concerning on this melancholy subject I was often a thing never understood rightly before, which is, that the men who are loudest in the cry of the growth of popery and the danger of the protestant religion are not really protestants, but a set of profligate men of no parts ... some learning and void of all principles, but pretend... ing to be republicans. I said that who told me this what I think much that these men so zealous about protecting the protestant religion seeing they are not Xtians? I was answered, that it was in order to recomend themselves to the Ministry, or if they can but work themselves or get themselves chosen Members of Parliament, will be sure to provide amply for them and the motive to their extraordinary zeal I was told is, that they thereby procure to themselves the connivance at least, if not the protection of the government, while they are propagating their Impiety and Infidelity. I hope in god this is not at so low an ebb in this country as this account I have had represents it to be, yet when I compare what I have formerly seen and heard at Rome with some things I have observed since I have been here, I am affraid there is too much truth in it.

The Bps are as unfair and partial in representing the security of their property as that of their religion, for when they mention it they dont say a word of the vast load of debt thats increasing yearly, under which the nation is groaning, and which must be paid if ever they intend to pay it, out of their property. Its true all this debt has not been contracted under the princes of this family... years of a profound peace which the nation has enjoyd, had it not been for the immense sums that have been ... away in corrupting Parliaments and supporting foreign Interests that can never be of any service to these Kingdoms.

I am affraid I have taken up too much of your Matys time about these sorry Mandates, but having mentioned them I was willing to give your Maty my sense of them. I remember Dr Wagstaff (with whom I wish I had conversed more frequently for he always told me truth) once said to me that I must not Judge of the Clergy of the Church of England by the Bps who were not promoted for their piety and learning, but for very different talents, viz for writing Pamphlets, for being active at Elections, and voting in Parliament as the Ministers directed them. After that I won another battle they'l write for me and answer their own letters.

There is another body of men amongst whom I am inclined to believe the lowest are the honestest as well as among the Clergy, I mean the Army. The common soldier was a body of men I looked then those I fought with this morning; yet they did not behave so well as I expected, I thought it would see plainly that the common men did not like the cause they were engaged in. Had they been fighting against frenchmen come to invade their country I am convinced they would make a bolder defence. The poor men's pay and their forage... that is not sufficient to corrupt their natural principles of Justice and honesty, which is not the case with their officers, who spoiled by their ambition and false notions of honor fought more desperately. I asked one of them who is my Prisoner a gallant man why he would fight so bravely against his lawfull Prince and one who was come to rescue his country from a foreign yoke? he said he was a man of honour and would be true to the Prince whose bread he ate and whose Commission he bore. I told him it was a noble principle but ill apply'd and asked him if he was not a Whig? he reply'd that he was, upon that I how come you to look on the connexion you bear and the bread you eat to be the principle and not your country which raises you and pays you to defend it against foreigners who come not to defend but to enslave it? For that I have ... understood to be the principles of a whig. Have you not heard how your countrymen have been coaxed abroad to be insulted and maltreated by those ... depredations and ... fighting in a quarrel in which your country has little or no concern only to enrich and aggrandize a... To all this he made no answer but looked sullen and hung down his head. The truth is, there are few good officers among them: they are brave because an Englishman cannot be otherwise, but they have generally little knowledge in their business, are corrupted in their morals, and have few restraints from religion; for they would have you believe you are fighting for it. As to their honor they talk so much of I shall soon have occasion to try it, for having no strong places to put my prisoners in, I shall be obliged to release them upon their parole. If they are not keep it, I wish they may not fall into my hands again, for in that case it will not be in my power to protect them from the resentment of my Highlanders who would be apt to kill them in cold blood, which as I take no pleasure in revenge would be extreamly shocking to me. My Lawfly Foe thinks it beneath him, I suppose, to settle a Cartel I wish for it as much for the sake of his men as my own. I hope ere its long it shall make him glad to sue for it. I hear there are one 6000 Dutch Troops arrived and some 10 Batts of the English sent for, I wish they were all Dutch that I might not have the pain of shedding English blood, however I shall... I shall soon oblige them to bring over the rest, which at all events will be one piece of service done my country in helping to keep it out of a ruinous foreign War.

'Tis hard my destiny should put me under new difficulties I did not feel before, and yet this is the case. I am now charged with the cares both ... of my friends and my enemys, for ... who should own the dead are run away, as if it was no business of theirs; and my Highlanders think it beneath them to do it, and the country people are fled away, however I am resolved to try if I can get people for money to undertake it, for I cannot bear the thoughts of suffering Englishmen to rot above ground. I am in a greater difficulty about what to do of my wounded prisoners!

Sir, since my landing everything has succeeded to meet
my wishes, it has pleased God to prosper me hitherto even
beyond my expectation. I have got together about 3000 (and am
promised more), brave and determined men who are resolved to
die or conquer with me. The enemy marched a body of regular
troops to attack me but when they came near they changed their
mind by taking a different route and making forced marches
they have escaped into the north to the great disappointment
of my highlanders: but I am not at all sorry for it, I shall
have the greater glory by beating them when they are more
numerous and supported by their dragoons. I have occasion to
reflect every day upon your majesty's last words to me, viz
[namely] that I would find power if it was not accompanied with
justice and clemency, an uneasy thing to myself and grievous
to those under me. 'Tis owing to the observance of this rule
and my conforming myself to the customs of those people that
I have got their hearts to a degree not to be easily conceived
by those who do not see it. One who observes the discipline
I have established would take my little army to be a body of
picked veterans; and to see the love and harmony that reigns
amongst us, he would be apt to look upon it as a large well-
ordered family in which everyone loves another better than
himself. I keep my health better in these wild mountains than
I used to do, in the campagnie felice [happy company], and
sleep sounder lying on the ground than I used to do in the
palaces at Rome. There is one thing and but one, in which I
have had any difference with my faithful highlanders, it was
about setting a price upon my kinsman's head, which knowing
your majesty's generous humanity I am sure will shock you as
much as it did me, when I was shown the proclamation setting a
price on my head. I smiled and treated it with the disdain it
deserved, upon which they flew out into a most violent rage and
insisted on my doing the same by him as this flowed solely from
the poor men's love and concern for me. I did not know how to
be angry with them for it, but tried to bring them to temper
by representing to them that it was a mean and barbarous
practice among princes that must dishonour them in the eyes of
all men of honour, that I could not see how my cousin having
set me the example would justify me in imitating that which
I blame so much in him. But nothing I could say would satisfy
them, some went even so far as to say, shall we go and venture
our lives for a man who seems so indifferent about preserving
his own? Thus I have been drawn in to do a thing for which

I can damn myself. Your majesty knows that in my nature I am
neither cruel or revengeful and God who knows my heart knows
that if the very prince who has forced me to this (for it is
he that has forced me) was in my power, the greatest pleasure
I could feel would be treating him as the brave, black Prince
treated his prisoner, the king of France, to make him ashamed
of having shown himself so inhumane an enemy to a man for
attempting a thing which he himself if he has any [sincerity]
would despise for not attempting. I beg your majesty would
be under no uneasiness about me, he is safe that's in God's
keeping: if I die it shall be as I have lived, with honour;
and the pleasure I take in thinking I have a brother in all
respects more worthy than myself to support your just cause,
and rescue my injur'd country from the oppression under which
it groans (if it will suffer itself to be rescued) makes life
more indifferent to me. As I know and admire the fortitude
with which your Majesty has supported your misfortunes, and
the generous disdain with which you have rejected all offers
of foreign assistance on terms which you thought dishonourable
to your self and injurious to your country; if our but
interested friends should at this time take advantage of the
tender affection with which they know you love me, I hope you
will reject them with the same magnanimity you have hitherto
shown, and leave me to shift for myself, as Edward the 3rd
left his brave son when he was in danger of being opress'd
by numbers in the field. No, Sir let it never be said that
to save your son you injur'd your country. When your enemies
bring in foreigners, and you reject all foreign assistance on
dishonourable terms, your deluded subjects of England must
see who is the true father of the people. For my own part,
I declare once and for all that while I breathe I will never
consent to alienate one foot of land that belongs to the Crown
of England, or set my hand to any treaty inconsistent with
its independency and sovereignty. If the English would have my
life, let them take it if they can. But no unkindness on their
part shall ever force me to a thing that may justify them in
taking it. I may be overcome by my enemies, but I will not
dishonour myself. If I die it shall be with my sword in hand
fighting for the reaction of those who fight against me. I know
there will be fulsome addresses from the different Corporations
of England; but I hope they will impose upon none but the
lower and more ignorant people. They will no doubt endeavour
to revive all the errors and excesses of my grandfather's

unhappy reign, and impute them to your Majesty and me, who had no hand in them, and suffered most by them. Can anything be more unreasonable than to suppose that your Majesty, who is so sensible of, and has so often considered the fatal errors of your father, would with your eyes open go and repeat them again?

Notwithstanding the repeated assurance your Majesty has given in your declaration that you will not invade any man's property, they endeavour to persuade that unthinking people that one of the first things they are to expect will be to see the public credit destroyed, as if it would be your interest to render yourself contemptible in the eyes of all the national of Europe and all the kingdoms you hope to reign over, poor at home and insignificant abroad. They no doubt try to frighten the present possessors of Church and Abbey lands with vain terrors as if your Majesty's intention was to resume them all, not considering that you have lived too long in a Catholick country and read the history of England too carefully not to have observed the many melancholy monuments to be seen there of the folly of those pious princes, who, thinking to honour religion, have lessened it by keeping superstitious rites in the Church, whereby they have insensibly rais'd up a power which has too often proved an overmatch for their succession.

I find it a great loss the brave Lord Marischal is not with me, his character is very high in this country, as it must be wherever he is known, I'd rather see him than 1000 French, who if they should come only as friends to assist your majesty in the recovery of your just right, the weak people would believe they came as invaders. There is one man of this country, who I would wish to have my friend, and that is the Duke of Argyll who I find is in high credit among them on account of his great ability and good qualities and had many dependants by his large fortune: but I am told I can hardly flatter myself with the hopes of it, the hard usage which his family received from ours sunk deep in his mind. What have those princes to answer for who by their cruelty have raised enemies not only to themselves but their innocent children, I must not close this letter without doing justice to your majesty's Protestant subjects, who I find are fully as zealous in your cause as the Roman Catholics, which is what honest Dr Wagstaff has often told me I would find when I can to try them. I design to march from hence tomorrow and I hope my next shall be from Edinburgh.

The routes followed by Charles Edward Stuart in 1743.

A family get-together
Prison governor's report on a family visit to Diana Mosley

5 DECEMBER 1941

This report from the governor of HM Prison Holloway, Doris Andrews, records a visit to Diana Mosley by her sister Unity Mitford and their mother, Lady Redesdale, on 5 December 1941. Diana, wife of Sir Oswald Mosley, had been detained under defence regulation 18B of the Defence of the Realm Act, 1939. The prison officers in attendance reported on the conversation to the governor, although as the governor states, this was difficult 'as Miss Mitford was very excited and spoke very quickly'.

In September 1939, on the outbreak of war, Unity – a devoted admirer of Hitler – had shot herself in the head in a botched suicide attempt. After treatment in Germany she had been repatriated via Switzerland in January 1940, but she was never the same again: the bullet remained lodged in her brain and was inoperable, which affected her personality, behaviour and reasoning thereafter. This was the illness discussed in the letter, and accounts for the illogical statement: 'I know why they won't put me in prison, it is because Winston Churchill knows that I committed suicide.'

It is not stated which of Diana's four sons – Jonathan and Desmond Guinness and Alexander and Max Mosley – were the two she adored and which the two she detested, though Oswald Mosley's sons are the ones most likely to be favoured. 'Des Romnelly' [sic] was Esmond Romilly, Unity and Diana's brother-in-law, married to their sister Jessica. He was a socialist (and former young Communist) and anti-Fascist serving with the RAF. Unknown to them at the time, he had been shot down and killed over the North Sea five days before, on 30 November 1941. Esmond's mother was the sister of Clementine Churchill, which made the British prime minister his uncle by marriage. Like her sister Unity (Bobo), Diana was pro-Fascist and had never met him: he had always refused to meet them.

The letter concludes on an optimistic note that Diana had heard from Tom (her husband, Oswald, was known as Tom) that they would soon be allowed to live together. This proved to be the case, since shortly afterwards Sir Oswald was allowed to move into a house in the grounds of Holloway prison and live there with Diana. They remained living in the grounds of Holloway until December 1943 when they were released on the orders of the Home Secretary, but were kept under house arrest in the country until the end of the war.

Such was her infamy as a Fascist sympathiser, Unity Mitford was persona non grata even at her younger sister's wedding.

COPY

From The Governor,
        H.M.Prison,
        Holloway.

                    5433 D.Mosley

        The above named was on 5.12.41 visited by her Mother
Lady Redesdale and the following is a copy of the report of
the visit for your information.

Sir,
        I beg to state that Reg.No. 5433 D.Mosley was visited
by her mother Lady Redesdale and Miss Unity Mitford; Miss Mitford was very excited, her conversation was about D.Mosley's
children; two she adores and detests the other two, her
family she spoke of each in turn, why she liked or disliked
them. Lady Redesdale appeared to be very amused at most
of her conversation. Miss Mitford said "I wish they would
put me in prison I should love to be herewith you". D.
Mosley said "I don't think they will do that, because you
are ill". Miss Mitford said "I don't look ill do I?" D.
Mosley said "No I think you look very well". Miss Mitford
said   " I know why they won't put me in prison, it is
because Winston Churchill knows that I committed suicide".
D.Mosley said "Never mind, when the war is over we can all
be happy again" Miss Mitford said "I know it will be over
in twelve months, I shall not tell you how I know, but I
am sure of it". Lady Redesdale spoke of her daughter who
has been ill, and also said how upset they all are at Des
Romilly being missing. D.Mosley said "I have never seen
him of course, he refuses ever to meet Bobo and Kit or I,
but of course I am very sorry because poor little Betty
was so fond of him. Did he come down in the sea". Miss
Mitford said "He came down on Berlin so there may be hopes
for him". Miss Mitford laughed for some time after this. D.
Mosley arranged with Lady Redesdale for her children's
Christmas, and told Lady Redesdale before leaving the things
would soon be better, as Tom had said in a letter yesterday
that something was being done re her husband being allowed
to live with her. The conversations at this visit were very
difficult to follow as Miss Mitford was very excited and
spoke very quickly and laughed a lot.
                            I am,Sir,
                    Yours obediently (sgd.) Doris Andrews,

Striving for *satyagraha*
Gandhi's letters to Sir Stafford Cripps

1946

By 1946, Indians had been campaigning for independence for many years and in Britain a Labour government under Clement Attlee was in power. Although the British government had not ruled out the possibility of maintaining its rule by force, it was apparent that the independence of India was close at hand. What was not clear, however, was the form that it would take. Mahatma Mohandas Karamchand Gandhi and The Indian National Congress with which he was associated sought a united independent India. On the other hand, Muhammed Ali Jinnah, leader of the Muslim League, was determined that Indian Muslims would not be subject to a Hindu-dominated state. This implied a separate, independent Pakistan.

These two letters from Gandhi to Sir Stafford Cripps were written in April 1946, during the British Cabinet Mission to India, which had arrived on 14 March. It aimed to resolve the difficult questions of Indian independence and to secure India's place within Britain's system of imperial defence. The Cabinet Mission was led by the Secretary of State for India and Burma, Lord Frederick Pethick-Lawrence, but Gandhi had a closer relationship with another of its members, Sir Stafford Cripps, whom he had met during Cripps's unsuccessful mission to India in 1942. This is evident in the correspondence between Gandhi and Cripps, since it has a very personal tone.

Gandhi was committed to an independent, democratic India undivided along religious lines. He was also committed to *satyagraha*, the use of non-violent means to achieve political ends; he abhorred the use of political violence. Having initiated the Quit India movement in August 1942 and subsequently spent two years as an internee, he also wanted a rapid end to British rule in India.

In this personal letter to Cripps, Gandhi confirmed that he would attend the conference at Simla, where the Cabinet Mission would advance proposals for a tiered federal government. While discussing the arrangements for his visit, Gandhi expressed uneasiness at the situation before the conference and felt that 'something is wrong'. He was probably concerned about the lack of progress or agreement in negotiations about the Mission's proposals for either a united federal India or an independent Pakistan.

This phase of the discussions also failed to produce agreement between the Mission, Congress and the League. Nevertheless, on 16 May, the Cabinet Mission

Gandhi outside 10 Downing Street.

issued a statement in the House of Commons proposing a united India, but with all governmental powers apart from foreign affairs, defence and communications resting with provincial governments. India should immediately move to an interim government and establish a representative constituent assembly to decide on a new constitution. Jinnah and the League accepted the 16 May proposal, but it was rejected by Congress.

Gandhi was disappointed by the outcome. In a statement of 26 May, he said that: '... We are far from the popular government at the Centre ... One would have thought that they would have formed the Central Government before issuing the statement ... It is taking a long time coming, whilst the millions are starving for want of food and clothing.' Furthermore, he objected to the continued presence of British troops in India during the period of interim government.

A further proposal by the Cabinet Mission issued on 16 June for an interim coalition government was also rejected. This failure to reach agreement on a united India precipitated the eventual outcome of partition in August 1947.

Harijan Mandir

5 ; 4 : 46

Dear Sir Stafford

Many thanks for your affectionate letter. Sundhip has given me your message too. I am here at least till 16th instance at Maulana Sahel's request.

Yours sincerely

M K Gandhi

Harijan Mandir

5; 4; 46

Dear Sir Stafford

Many thanks for
your affectionate
letter. Sundhip has
given me your message
too. I am here at
least till 16th instance
at Mawlana Sahib's request.

Yours sincerely

M K Ghandhi

New Delhi
29 4 46

Dear Sir Stafford,

You do not understand
how uneasy I feel. Some
thing is wrong. But
I shall come to Simla.
I cannot take my ne-
cessarily big family to
Rajkumari's house.
I have to fall back
upon the Govt for
quarters for about
15 people. Hardly any
service will be wanted.
But utensils & foodstuff
will be necessary. Goats
milk. And train
accommodation
& the lift from Kalka.
All this is strange
for me but it has
become true.

Yours sincerely
MKGandhi

New Delhi

19 4 46

Dear Sir Stafford

You do not understand
how uneasy I feel. Some
thing is wrong. But
I shall come to Simla.
I cannot take my
necessarily big family to
Rajkuman's house.
I have to fall back
upon the Govt for
quarters for about
15 people. Hardly any
service will be wanted.
But utensils & food stuff
will be necessary. Goats
milk. And train
accommodation
& the lift from Kalka.
All this is strange
for me but it has become true.

Yours sincerely
M K Ghandhi

India's plan for uniting and merging Indian states, 1948.

Gandhi and a large peaceful crowd engaging in an act of civil disobedience.

An attempt to assuage fears of immigration
Clement Attlee to Labour MPs on the arrival of *Empire Windrush*

5 JULY 1948

On 21 June 1948, the steamer *Empire Windrush* docked at Tilbury, near London. Aboard the ship were 492 Jamaican passengers, coming to Britain to look for work and a new life. These were the first of the so-called *Windrush* generation of Caribbean migrants to Britain who, along with their descendants, have shaped British society in the 70 years since the ship docked.

Attitudes towards immigration to Britain of people from the Caribbean have not always been the same, and at the time the *Windrush*'s arrival caused something akin to a moral panic, not least in the House of Commons. Shortly after the migrants arrived, eleven Labour MPs wrote to their party leader and Prime Minister, Clement Attlee, raising concerns:

'An influx of coloured people domiciled here is likely to impair the harmony, strength and cohesion of our public and social life and to cause discord and unhappiness among all concerned.'

This letter, Attlee's reply of 5 July, two weeks after the *Windrush* docked, gives the Prime Minister's somewhat lukewarm defence of the migrants' rights and integrity, writing to his colleagues: 'I think it would be a great mistake to take the emigration of this Jamaican party to the United Kingdom too seriously ... The majority of them are honest workers, who can make a genuine contribution'. Furthermore, he wrote, the Jamaicans aboard the *Windrush* had every right to live and work in the UK, as British Colonial subjects and citizens (it was not until 1962 that immigration from the Commonwealth was restricted). It was traditional, said Attlee, and that tradition was 'not, in my view, to be lightly discarded'.

Overall, Attlee's letter strives to present an air of calm detachment from the issue, saying that 'too much importance – too much publicity too – has been attached to the present argosy of Jamaicans'. his aloofness however, belies the frantic machinations of government as the *Windrush* approached Britain. Telegrams concerning the *Windrush* were exchanged with Colonial officials in Jamaica and the Colonies Secretary prepared a briefing for Cabinet on the migrants aboard. In response to the concerns that were raised about where those men without work or lodgings would go on arrival, 'suitable'

Some of the men who travelled to England on the *Windrush*.

Clement Attlee was prime minister from 1945 until 1951.

accommodation was found for 236 of the 492: a deep, cramped air-raid shelter under Clapham South Underground Station that had no hot water.

Events seem to have transpired somewhat differently from the government and Attlee's correspondents' expectations. Having worried about the men's character before their arrival, the Ministry of Labour soon reported that they were 'on the whole rather better than the type we had anticipated'. As Attlee reports in this letter, the *Windrush*'s passengers quickly found work and moved from the shelter.

Attlee wrote his letter on a significant day – 5 July 1948 – the day the National Health Service treated its first patients. The NHS's establishment was a momentous event, as was the arrival of the first of many Caribbean people aboard the *Windrush*. For, while Attlee wrote that he thought 'a similar large influx' from Jamaica unlikely, he was wrong: many thousands more travelled to Britain from the Caribbean and, although they faced great hardships and discrimination, stayed.

The *Empire Windrush* arriving from Jamaica on 21 June 1948.

10 Downing Street
S.W.1

5th July, 1948

I am replying to the letter signed by yourself
and ten other Members of Parliament on the 22nd of
June about the West Indians who arrived in this
country on that day on board the "Empire Windrush".
I note what you say, but I think it would be a great
mistake to take the emigration of this Jamaican party
to the United Kingdom too seriously.

It is traditional that British subjects, whether
of Dominion or Colonial origin (and of whatever race
or colour), should be freely admissible to the
United Kingdom. That tradition is not, in my view, to
be lightly discarded, particularly at a time when we
are importing foreign labour in large numbers. It
would be fiercely resented in the Colonies themselves,
and it would be a great mistake to take any measure

which .....

which would tend to weaken the goodwill and loyalty
of the Colonies towards Great Britain. If our policy
were to result in a great influx of undesirables, we
might, however unwillingly, have to consider modifying
it. But I should not be willing to consider that
except on really compelling evidence, which I do not
think exists at the present time. We have not yet
got complete figures on the disposal of the party which
arrived on the "Empire Windrush", but it may be of
interest to you to know that of the 256 who had
nowhere to go and no immediate prospects of employment,
and who were therefore temporarily accommodated at
Clapham Shelter, 145 had actually been placed in
employment by the 30th June and the number still
resident in the Shelter at this last week-end was down
to 76. It would therefore be a great mistake to
regard these people as undesirables or unemployables.
The majority of them are honest workers, who can make

a .....

a genuine contribution to our labour difficulties at
the present time.

You and your fellow signatories say that Colonial
Governments are responsible for the welfare of their
peoples. That is true, and all the Colonial
Governments have their ten-year plans of development,
assisted from the Colonial Development and Welfare
Act of the United Kingdom. But they, like this country,
are embarrassed by shortages of materials and shortages
of skilled directing personnel as well as to some
extent by the universal dollar shortage. These
factors prevent them driving ahead as fast as they
and we would wish.

It is difficult to prophesy whether events will
repeat themselves, but I think it will be shown that
too much importance - too much publicity too - has
been attached to the present argosy of Jamaicans.
Exceptionally favourable shipping terms were available

to .....

to them, and there was a large proportion of
them who had money in their pockets from their
ex-service gratuities. These circumstances are
not likely to be repeated; yet even so not all the
passages available were taken up.

It is too early yet to assess the impression
made upon these immigrants as to their prospects
in Great Britain and consequently the degree to
which their experience may attract others to follow
their example. Although it has been possible to
find employment for quite a number of them, they may
well find it very difficult to make adequate
remittances to their dependants in Jamaica as well as
maintaining themselves over here. On the whole,
therefore, I doubt whether there is likely to be a
similar large influx.

(SIGNED) C.R. ATTLEE

J.D. Murray, Esq., M.P.

'The greatest and most horrible crime'
Churchill on the mass deportations of Hungarian Jewry

JULY 1944

In March 1944, Foreign Secretary Anthony Eden declared in the House of Commons that there was compelling evidence that the Nazi policy of extermination of Jews had not been halted – an announcement that had been prompted by concerns voiced by the Jewish Agency following the invasion of Hungary by the Nazis earlier that month. This had arisen after Hitler had given the Hungarian regent, Miklós Horthy, a choice to run a Quisling government or else be under German occupation. Horthy had been persuaded to choose the former option and had returned to Hungary from his meeting with Hitler in Salzburg on the same day that the German Army entered Hungary. A few days later, Adolf Eichmann left his desk job in Berlin and arrived in Budapest to implement a new government and oversee the destruction of Hungarian Jewry. Hungary's ambassador to Germany, Döme Sztójay, was appointed prime minister and other known anti-Semites were given key administrative roles.

Eichmann's experience in organising ghettos and deportations and dealing with uprisings made him the obvious choice to oversee the installation of a Jewish Council for the purpose of keeping the Jewish population calm by lying to them about the Nazi plans for the Hungarian Jews. The Germans were in need of forced labour and with the Soviet Army advancing, it was believable for the Hungarian Jews to think that the war would soon be over and that indeed they would be spared: though the invasion was very alarming, the idea of mass deportations to death camps was not necessarily seen by them as inevitable.

Winston Churchill.

The first transport left Budapest for Auschwitz-Birkenau on 15 May 1944. The Jews found themselves arriving and disembarking on a recently improved platform, situated closer to the four gas chambers and crematoria. Only around twenty-five per cent of the arrivals were selected on the ramp for slave labour, with the remaining Jews being sent to their deaths within an hour of their arrival. It is estimated that 440,000 Hungarian Jews were murdered in the gas chambers in Auschwitz-Birkenau.

On 4 July 1944 the Foreign Office received a summary from the Czechoslovakian government, which was operating in exile from London. Written by two Jewish escapees of Auschwitz, Vrba and Wetzler, the report described conditions in the camps of Auschwitz and Auschwitz-Birkenau and named Auschwitz-Birkenau as the destination to which the Hungarian Jews were being deported. It was this information that prompted Chaim Weizmann, president of the World Zionist Organisation and future president of Israel, to appeal to the Allies to bomb the railway lines that ran from Budapest to Auschwitz.

Although this idea had previously been considered and dismissed, Eden was willing to re-examine it and told Churchill of Weizmann's proposal. On 7 July, Eden at once wrote only to the Air Ministry, seeking out their views on such a plan and bypassing the Cabinet – at Churchill's suggestion.

However, within days of this letter being sent the deportations were halted: the last mass deportation of Hungarian Jews occurred on 8 July, news of which was reported by the Foreign Office on 18 July. Nevertheless, throughout July Allied bombing raids on German industrial plants continued, but with heavy losses. On the bombing of railway lines leading to the camps, the Air Ministry reported to Eden that 'the distance of Silesia from our bases entirely rules out doing anything of the kind'. The proposal of bombing the camps had already been rejected by the Americans some weeks before.

On 13 July, Churchill composed a reply to a letter from the Archbishop of Canterbury reiterating that the world had witnessed 'the greatest and most horrible crimes ever committed' and that 'the principal hope of terminating this tragic state of affairs must remain a speedy victory of the Allied Nations'.

COPY   10 Downing Street,

                                            Whitehall, S.W.1.

PRIVATE   13 July, 1944

My dear Henry,

        You wrote to me on 1 July about the German plans for the
massacre of the Hungarian Jews.

        I have forwarded your letter to the Foreign Secretary and
fear that I can add nothing to the statement he made in the House on
5 July in replying to Silverman's Question.

        There is no doubt in my mind that we are in the presence of
one of the greatest and most horrible crimes ever committed. It has
been done by scientific machinery by nominally civilized men in the name
of a great state and one of the leading races of Europe. I need not
assure you that the situation has received and will receive the most
earnest consideration from my colleagues and myself but, as the
Foreign Secretary said, the principal hope of terminating it must remain
the speedy victory of the Allied Nations.

                        Yours sincerely,

                            (sd) WINSTON S. CHURCHILL

The Lord Melchett.

PRIME MINISTER'S
PERSONAL MINUTE
10. Downing Street,
Whitehall.

WR 274

SERIAL No. M.844/4

134

FOREIGN SECRETARY.

There is no doubt that this is probably
the greatest and most horrible crime ever committed
in the whole history of the world, and that it has
been done by scientific machinery by nominally civilized
men in the name of a great State and one of the leading
races of Europe. It is quite clear that all concerned
in this crime who may fall into our hands, including
the people who only obeyed orders by carrying out the
butcheries, should be put to death after their
association with the murders has been proved.

I cannot therefore feel that this is the
kind of ordinary case which is put through the Protecting Power as, for instance, the lack of feeding
or sanitary conditions in some particular prisoners'
camp. There should therefore in my opinion be no
negotiations of any kind on this subject. Declarations
should be made in public, so that everyone connected
with it will be hunted down and put to death.

2.   The project which has been put forward

- 2 -   135

through a very doubtful channel seems itself also
to be of the most nondescript character. I would
not take it seriously.

W.

11.7.44.

Ref: P.M./44/499

Chewing the fat
Princess Margaret exchanges views with Margaret Thatcher

7 FEBRUARY 1980

One was the middle-class daughter of a greengrocer who trained as a chemist before becoming a barrister and moving into the male-dominated world of politics. The other was a princess born into the House of Windsor at Glamis Castle, who was educated at home by her governess before becoming a well-known socialite and party-goer. Yet despite this, by early 1980 the pair had become unlikely pen pals: one as Britain's first female prime minister, the other as younger sister to Queen Elizabeth II.

These extraordinary, chatty handwritten letters between Margaret Thatcher and Princess Margaret offer a rare glimpse into the personal interaction between a prime minister and a senior royal in the twentieth century, revealing their chiming views on international and domestic affairs. Writing eight months into her first term as prime minister, Thatcher opens her letter by revealing how distressed she was to hear that the princess had been in hospital. She then goes on to mention their respective recent visits to the USA, and describes how the US hostage situation in Iran 'dominated every conversation' she had in Washington and New York, while the Soviet Union invasion of Afghanistan had 'cast a shadow over the whole world'.

Back in the UK, the Conservative government was grappling with a steelworkers' strike in January 1980, and Thatcher in her letter admits difficulty in getting 'across the message that more money has to be earned and not just demanded'. The princess offers her perspective on the situation, as we can see in the letter shown here, by replying: 'I suppose if one is an ordinary working man and one's union tells one not to vote for new machinery or technology because otherwise you will lose your job or your card – you just don't dare.'

Penning her response from Kensington Palace on notepaper headed with a crowned 'M' monogram, Princess Margaret's lively letter covers a range of topics. Addressing Thatcher as 'My dear Prime Minister', Margaret starts by thanking Thatcher for the 'kind letter' enquiring after her health and revealing rather candidly: 'I just had to have some things dug out of my face but everything went well.'

On Soviet intentions in Afghanistan, Princess Margaret enquires whether the invasion could be a precursor to an attack on neighbouring Iran to 'get all the oil'. Soviet action had led the White House to propose a boycott of that summer's Olympic Games in

Russian athletes carrying doves as they march at the 1980 Moscow Olympics.

Princess Margaret on a visit to Germany in March, 1980.

Moscow, with boxing legend Muhammad Ali being used to lobby for support in several African countries. An uncompromising, if also unkind, Margaret notes that in a Cold War world of superpower politics: 'If that silly boxer doesn't make a hash of it he might get Africa to cock a snook at the Russians.' In the end, sixty-six invited nations did not attend the Games for various reasons – including nineteen from Africa.

PM Passport

♔
KENSINGTON PALACE

February 7
1980

My dear Prime Minister,

I write belatedly to thank you for your kind letter. I just had to have some thing dug out of my face but luckily everything went well and wasn't worrying.

I was so interested to hear about your visit to the United States. I expect you surprised them no end at answering their questions in a positive way, when they are

cock a snook at the Russians. I find it quite impossible to find out **What** is happening in Afghanistan. Are they are about to wheel into Iran and get all the oil? More power to your policy of nuclear power stations. I wish they weren't called "nuclear" as people always think of the bomb. I've been advocating them since I was 20!

Many thanks for allocating £10,000 to the N.S.P.C.C. They are vital and I am President and support their free service.

With again many thanks for your letter

Yours very sincerely

Margaret

February 7

1980

My dear Prime Minister

                    I write belatedly to thank you
for your kind letter. I just had to have some things
dug out of my face but luckily everything went well
and weren't worrying.

I was so interested to hear about your visit to the
United States. I expect you surprised him no end at
answering their questions in a positive way, when
they are used to waffling on for hours in figures of 8,
not actually answering anything.

The steel strike is depressing. I well remember when
Charles Villiers took it over. I congratulated him on
his courage and he said, "I am taking on a moribund,
old fashioned, out of date, uneconomical, out of date
industry" and I said "Is there any hope of improving
it?" and he said "Very little".

I suppose if one is an ordinary working man and one's
union tells one not to vote for new machinery or
technology because otherwise you will lose your job
or your card — you just don't dare.

I went to Cambridge for a Debate (rather dull, all
about the church, lots of clerics) and find them all
rabid conservatives — not a Trotskyite to argue with!
They were passionately against the Olympic Games in
Moscow. I tried the "Isn't it hard on the athletes"
bit but they were adamant. I suppose individuals
must choose whether to go as it's up to the Olympic
Committee. If that silly boxer doesn't make a hash
of it he might get Africa to cock a snook at the
Russians.

I find it quite impossible to find out what is
happening in Afghanistan. Are they about to wheel
into Iran and get all the oil? More power to your
policy of nuclear power stations. I wish they weren't
called "nuclear" as people always think of the bomb.
I've been advocating this since I was 20!

Many thanks for allocating £10,000 to the NSPCC. They
are vital and I am President and support their free
service.

With again many thanks for your letter
            Yours very sincerely
                Margaret

A fond farewell
Mikhail Gorbachev to Margaret Thatcher on her resignation

22 NOVEMBER 1990

This document is a letter from Mikhail Gorbachev to Margaret Thatcher, dated 22 November 1990 – the day on which she announced she was stepping down as prime minister. Addressing her as 'Dear Margaret' for the very first time, the Soviet leader sends his best wishes in an uncharacteristically warm and friendly tone, while also reminding Thatcher that his 'international activities (...) [had] started with their conversations as far back as 1984'.

When he visited the UK in 1984, heading a Soviet parliamentary delegation, Gorbachev was nothing more than the rising star of the Politburo. Despite this, he spent hours with Margaret Thatcher, discussing a broad range of topics: East/West relations, nuclear weapons, security, human rights, the miners' strike and economic and social issues. The two leaders had gone on to develop a 'mutual understanding' that lasted throughout their professional relationship. Margaret Thatcher later described the visit as 'an outstanding international success'. For Gorbachev, it had been the first opportunity to display the political line he would follow – that of a rather atypical Soviet official, who nevertheless remained loyal to the system.

Gorbachev was part of a 'new generation' of Soviet leaders: he hadn't been born when Lenin had died, he hadn't held any position under Stalin, and the first Party Congress he attended as a Komsomol delegate was the twentieth, in 1956, during which Khrushchev denounced Stalin in his famous 'secret speech'. When he was elected as general secretary of the Communist Party of the Soviet Union on 11 March 1985, he became the youngest leader the USSR had ever had – the youngest and the last. His line, however, was one of soft continuity rather than radical generational change: he wanted to reform the system from within, to make it better, more suited to the world it had to face, without getting rid of it altogether.

Margaret Thatcher.

Mikhail Gorbachev.

Gorbachev certainly displayed a shift in thinking, but the very terms 'perestroika' ('restructuring', as in restructuring the political and economic system), 'demokratizatsiya' ('democratisation', as in authorising multi-candidate elections), 'uskoreniye' ('acceleration', as in accelerating the social and economic development) and 'glasnost' ('transparency', as in achieving more transparency in government institutions and activities) remained in line with the usual ideological discourse.

The ideological differences between Thatcher and Gorbachev were very clear. What's more, they were both deeply committed to their own values and political systems, which could have made the relationship difficult. For instance, they had an irreconcilable difference of opinion on nuclear weapons: she believed they were a deterrent, and therefore necessary, whereas he raised the spectre of a nuclear winter, and wanted to ban at least some of them – a view that led to the 1987 Intermediate-Range Nuclear Forces Treaty (INF). Margaret Thatcher, however, famously told BBC's John Cole: 'I like Mr Gorbachev. We can do business together.'

When he wrote this letter in November 1990, Mikhail Gorbachev, who would himself step down in December 1991, knew the world was drastically different. The Berlin Wall had fallen, Germany was reunified, the Soviet Union was living its last moments – the Cold War was over. It is perhaps therefore not so surprising that Margaret Thatcher, in her reply, wrote warmly and somewhat longingly: 'together we really did contribute to changing our world.'

The Rt.Hon. Mrs.Margaret Thatcher, MP
Prime-Minister
10, Downing Str.
London

Dear Margaret,

I have just learned of your decision to leave
the post of the leader of the Conservative party
and Prime-Minister of Great Britain.

It is with the feeling of great warmth and
deep satisfaction that I recall all our businesslike talks that played such a great role in the
development of the relations between the Soviet
Union and Great Britain. I highly appreciate the
mutual understanding on many issues that has developed between us. It is also symbolic for me that
my international activities had in practice started
with our conversations as far back as 1984.

Every politician is appraised both in his own
time and by the future. I have no doubts that as
a political leader you have made an enormous contribution both into the history of Great Britain and
the world community at large.

      I hope for the continuation of our friendly meetings.

      Raisa Maximovna joins me in all heartfelt greetings to you.

      Our warmest regards to Denis.

      Yours respectfully,

                       M.Gorbachev

22 November 1990

MARTY
DE MISS

REM

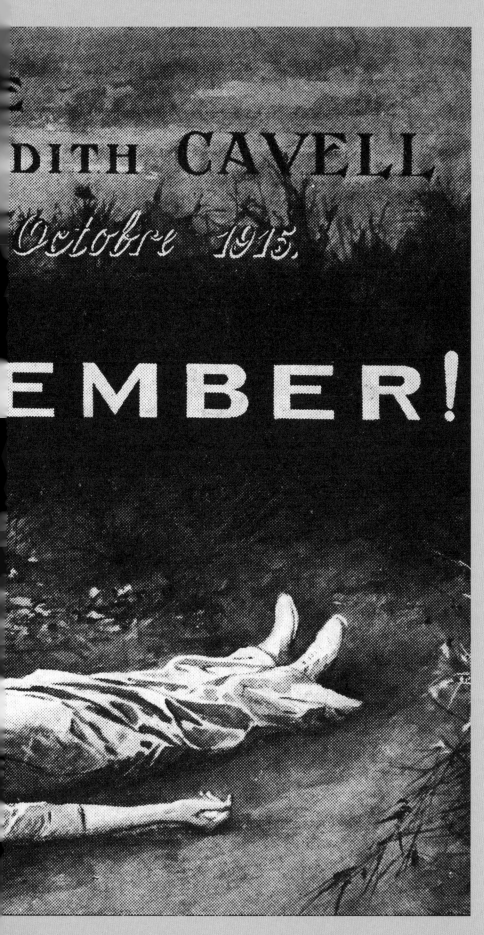

Expeditions, foreign
policy and espionage

Brutal attack on the road to Timbuktu
Letter from Major Alexander Gordon Laing to Hanmer Warrington

10 MAY 1826

This document is a letter from Major Alexander Gordon Laing to Hanmer Warrington, the British consul general at Tripoli. Writing on 10 May 1826, he describes very vividly the injuries he received during a Tuareg attack as he was on his way to Timbuktu.

Laing had left Britain in February 1825 to gather information on the Niger basin and determine the exact location of Timbuktu, in present-day Mali – a city that at the time was still semi-mythical and that no European had ever reached from the north. He arrived in Tripoli in May, fell in love with Emma Warrington, the consul's daughter, and, after a whirlwind romance, married her on 14 July.

A few days after his wedding, Laing set out for Timbuktu under the guidance of Shaykh Babani. Having travelled across the Sahara, he reached Ghadames, in the west of present-day Libya, in October, then In Salah, in present-day Algeria, in December. In January 1826, Laing and his party left In Salah and started marching across the Tanezrouft desert, which is when the attack occurred.

In his letter, Laing describes the incident as 'base treachery' and implies the Shaykh might have been partly responsible for it. He doesn't describe the attack itself, but from the number of wounds he sustained, and the severity of them, it must have been savage. Writing with his left hand, as his right hand had been 'cut three fourths across', he explains he had received twenty-four wounds, 'eighteen of which are exceedingly severe'. He had numerous sabre cuts all over his head, face, arms and legs, multiple open fractures, and a musket ball in his hip that had 'made its way through [his] back, slightly grazing the back bone'. After the attack was over he had been left for dead.

Alexander Gordon Laing.

Against all odds, he somehow managed to survive both the attack and the 400-mile journey to Shaykh Sidi Muhammad's territory, from where he was writing. 'I am nevertheless, as I have already said, doing well', he assured Warrington with either great courage, foolish bravado, or a bit of both.

He was determined to press on and reach Timbuktu, and was also eager to collect more geographical information as he had found en route that 'the map indeed [required] much correction'.

Laing finally reached Timbuktu on 13 August 1826. Writing to Warrington again on 21 September, he said the city had 'completely met [his] expectations', but that his position was rather unsafe due to the unfriendly disposition of the locals. He was anxious to leave, and hoped he could do so early in the morning of 22 August. Instead of trying to retrace his steps back to Tripoli, he said, he would proceed to Sego (present-day Ségou, in south-central Mali) – even though he knew it was a dangerous road.

This was the last Warrington was to hear from his son-in-law. A few days after his departure from Timbuktu, Laing and his party were ambushed in Sahab, about thirty miles north – this time, he didn't survive. It wasn't until French explorer René Caillé entered the city in April 1828, two years later, that any European managed to reach Timbuktu (and return) alive.

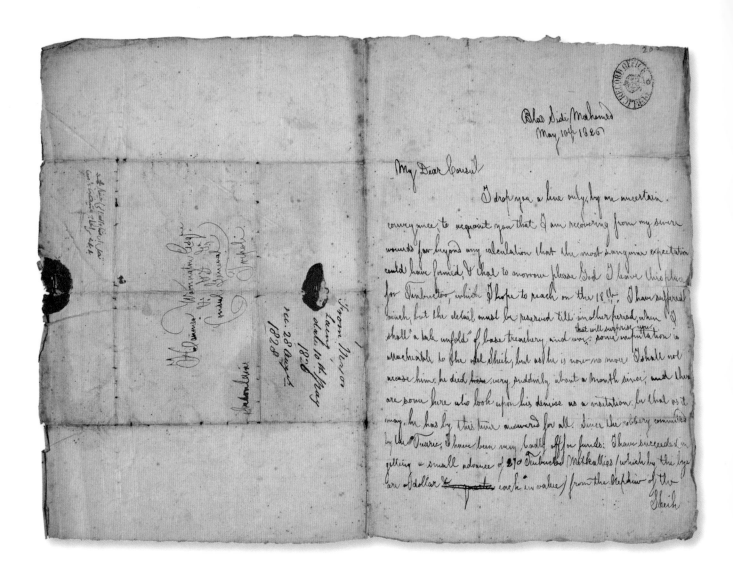

Blad Sidi Mahomed
May 10th 1826

My Dear Consul

I drop you a line only, by an uncertain
conveyance, to acquaint you that I am recovering from my severe
wounds far beyond any calculation that the most sanguine expectation
could have formed, & that to morrow please God I leave this place
for Timbuctoo, which I hope to reach on the 18th. I have suffered
much, but the detail must be reserved till another period, when I
shall "a tale unfold" of base treachery and woe, that will surprise you ~ some imputation is
attachable to Old Sheik, but as he is now no more I shall not
accuse him, he died here very suddenly, about a month since, and there
are some here who look upon his demise as a visitation; be that as it
may, he has by this time answered for all. Since the robbery committed
by the Tuaric, I have been very badly off for funds: I have succeeded in
getting a small advance of 270 Timbuctoo Mithcallies (which by the bye
are a dollar each in value) from the Nephew of the
                                                          Sheik

Sheik, who is a remarkably fine young man, & who has shewn me much
attention all along, but more particularly since the death of his uncle.
As he will carry my dispatches from Timbuctoo you will have an
opportunity of seeing him when I shall recommend him to your best
notice and attention — When I write from Timbuctoo, I shall detail
precisely how I was betrayed & nearly murdered in my sleep, in the
mean time I shall acquaint you with the number and nature of
my wounds, in all amounting to twenty four, eighteen of which are
exceedingly severe — To begin from the top, I have five sabre cuts
on the crown of the head & three on the left temple, all fractures
from which much bone has come away, one on my left cheek
which fractured the jaw bone, & has divided the ear, forming a very
unsightly wound, one over the right temple, and a dreadful gash on
the back of the neck, which slightly scratched the windpipe: a
musket ball in the hip, which made its way through my back slightly
grazing the back bone: five sabre cuts on my right arm & hand,
three of the fingers broken, the hand cut three fourths across, and
the wrist bones cut through; three cuts on the left arm, the bone of
which has been broken, but is again uniting. One slight wound on the
right

right leg, and two do with one dreadful gash on the left, to say
nothing of a cut across the fingers of my left hand now healed up. I
am nevertheless, as I have already said, doing well, and hope yet to return
to England with much important Geographical information. The map
indeed requires much correction, and please God, I shall get do much in
addition to what I have already done, towards putting it right —

So much is official & I shall feel obliged by your sending a copy of
it to Lord Bathurst, as I write with my left hand with much pain
and difficulty, and shall not upon that account communicate till my
arrival at Timbuctoo — Private I have many charges of complaint against
the memory of the late Sheik, all of which you shall know in due time —
he has never repaid the 400£ he borrowed from me at Ghadames, he
bore no expense of any sort upon the road, and when I was laying without
expectations of living he took my best gun, sent it to Timbuctoo & sold it
for a hundred dollars the original cost in England — I write to no one but
you; May God bless you all; I dare not yet trust myself with my
feelings, for which reason I have not attempted a line to my dearest
Emma; I shall make the trial at Timbuctoo, & in the mean time
remember me with kindest love, & beg her to think nothing of my
misfortunes, for all will yet be well —
Yours ever truly
A Gordon Laing

                          Blad Sidi Mahomed
                          May 10th 1826

My Dear Consul,

        I drop you a line only, by an uncertain conveyance,
to acquaint you that I am recovering from my severe wounds far
beyond any calculation that the most sanguine expectation could
have formed and that tomorrow please God I leave this place for
Timbuctoo, which I hope to reach on the 18th. I have suffered much,
but the detail must be reserved till another period, when I shall
"a tale unfold" of base treachery and war that will surprise you:
some imputation is attachable to the old Sheikh, but as he is now
no more I shall not accuse him: he died very suddenly about a
month since, and there are some here who look upon his demise as a
visitation: be that as it may, he has by this time answered for all.
Since the robbery committed by the Tuaric, I have been very badly
off for funds: I have succeeded in getting a small advance of 270
Timbuctoo Mitkallies (which by the by are a dollar and a quarter
each in value) from the nephew of the Sheikh, who is a remarkably
fine young man, and who has shown me much attention all along,
but more particularly since the death of his uncle. As he will
carry my despatches from Timbuctoo you will have an opportunity
of seeing him, when I shall recommend him to your best notice and
attention — When I write from Timbuctoo, I shall detail precisely
how I was betrayed and nearly murdered in my sleep in the mean
time I shall acquaint you with the number and nature of my wounds,
in all amounting to twenty four, eighteen of which are exceedingly
severe. To begin from the top, I have five sabre cuts on the crown
of the head and three on the left temple, all fractures from which
much bone has come away, one on my left cheek which fractured the
jaw bone, and has divided the ear, forming a very unsightly wound,
one over the right temple, and a dreadful gash on the back of the
neck, which slightly scratched the windpipe; a musket ball in the

hip, which made its way through my back, slightly grazing the back bone; five sabre cuts on my right arm and hand, three of the fingers broken, the hand cut three fourths across, and the wrist bones cut through; three cuts on the left arm, the bone of which has been broken, but is again writing. One slight wound on the right leg, and two ditto with one dreadful gash on the left, to say nothing of a cut across the fingers of my left hand, now healed up. I am nevertheless, as I have already said, doing well, and hope yet to return to England with much important Geographical information. The map indeed requires much correction, and please God, I shall yet do much in addition to what I have already done, towards putting it right.

So much is official, and I shall feel obliged by your sending a copy of it to Lord Bathurst, as I write with my left hand with much pain and difficulty and shall not upon that account communicate till my arrival at Timbuctoo. Private. I have many charges of complaint against the memory of the old Sheikh, all of which you shall know in due time. He has never repaid the 400$ he borrowed from me at Biniolud; he bore no expense of any sort upon the road and when I was laying without expectations of living, he took my last gun, sent it to Timbuctoo and sold it for a hundred dollars, the original cost in England. I write to no one but you; may God bless you all. I dare not yet trust myself with my feelings, for which reason I have not attempted a line to my dearest Emma: I shall make the trial at Timbuctoo, in the mean time remember me with kindest love, and I beg her to think nothing of my misfortune, for all will yet be well.

Yours ever truly,

(Signed) A Gordon Laing

The start of the 'special relationship'?
Abraham Lincoln writes to Queen Victoria requesting a royal visit

18 MAY 1863

In 1863 His Royal Highness Prince Albert, the Prince of Wales, son of Queen Victoria and Prince Albert, married Her Royal Highness the Princess Alexandra Caroline Maria Charlotte Lovita Julia, daughter of Prince Christian of Denmark. The ceremony took place in St George's Chapel, Windsor Castle on Tuesday 10 March 1863.

Queen Victoria was still mourning the loss of her husband, Prince Albert, and insisted on a smaller, less-public wedding, rather than a full state occasion.

Following the marriage in 1863, royal letters were sent to those who had not received an invitation. These numbered heads of states and leaders around the world, including emperors and empresses of Austria, Russia and Brazil; kings and queens of Bavaria, Belgium, Portugal and Spain; and senates of Peru, Costa Rica, Salvador and Frankfurt. Letters of congratulation were duly received from nations including Venezuela, the Argentine Republic, Chile and throughout Europe. These letters can be found in The National Archives.

This particular one shows the warmth and fondness the US president, Abraham Lincoln, had for the British royal family.

Back in Britain, as a result of Queen Victoria's long reign, Prince Albert was at that time England's longest-serving Prince of Wales. What's more, the Queen scorned the Prince's playboy lifestyle – he travelled extensively, enjoying his life as a bachelor – and had kept him out of political life.

This did not mean, however, that he performed no royal duties: in 1860, when Canada requested a royal visit in recognition of the fact that a Canadian regiment had fought for Britain in the Crimean War, it was he who was sent. Queen Victoria was not in favour of a tour: she neither wanted to cross the ocean, nor acknowledge Canada or the USA. Instead, swayed by the persuasive arguments of Prince Albert and the Duke of Newcastle, and seeing it as a means to occupy the eighteen-year-old Prince, Queen Victoria agreed to Albert going in her stead. On hearing about the tour of Canada, President James Buchanan requested that the Prince should extend the trip to include the USA, making this the first official royal tour of both nations.

Abraham Lincoln.

Starting the tour in Canada on 23 July 1860, Albert witnessed the country's deep and lasting attachment to both Queen and country. Crowds turned out in their thousands to see the young Prince who, among other things, opened the Victoria Bridge cross the St Lawrence River, Montreal.

Having crossed the border, the Prince was met with an equally warm welcome by the people of the USA. Arriving in Washington on 3 October 1860, he met President James Buchanan and stayed at the White House. He was also the first royal to visit Mount Vernon.

Elsewhere in the USA things were not so amicable: the presidential campaign of 1860 had highlighted the tensions between the northern and southern states, the rights of states, and the question of slavery. With these tensions growing, the Prince only visited as far south as Richmond, where he refused to visit slave quarters.

Shortly afterwards, in November 1860, Abraham Lincoln was elected president of the USA, and by April 1861 the country was at war.

In that same year Mary Lincoln renovated the White House and renamed a suite in the north-west corner the Prince of Wales Room. Following his assassination in April 1865, Abraham Lincoln was laid to rest and his autopsy was performed in this room.

The Prince of Wales and Princess Alexandra in 1862, before their wedding.

Abraham Lincoln,
President of the United States of America,

To Her Majesty Victoria,
        Queen of the United Kingdom
            of Great Britain and Ireland
                †.   †.   †. Sendeth Greeting!
Great and Good Friend:

        I have received the letter which Your Majesty
addressed to me on the 31st day of March last,
announcing the pleasing intelligence of the
marriage on the 10th of that month, of Your Majesty's
dearly beloved Son His Royal Highness Albert
Edward, Prince of Wales, Duke of Saxony, Prince of
Saxe=Coburg and Gotha, †. †. with Her Royal
Highness the Princess Alexandra Caroline Maria
Charlotte Louisa Julia, eldest Daughter of His
Royal Highness the Prince Christian of Denmark.
Feeling a lively interest in whatever concerns the
welfare and happiness of Your Majesty's
illustrious House, I pray Your Majesty to receive
my cordial congratulations on this auspicious
event, and my fervent wishes that it may signally

promote your own happiness and that of the Prince your Son and his young Spouse. And so I recommend Your Majesty and Your Majesty's Royal Family to the protection of the Almighty.

Written at Washington the 18th day of May, in the year of our Lord one thousand eight hundred and sixty-three.

Your Good Friend,

Abraham Lincoln

By the President:

William H. Seward
Secretary of State.

Abraham Lincoln

President of the United States of America

To Her Majesty Victoria
    Queen of the United Kingdom
        of Great Britain and Ireland, etc etc etc sendeth greeting

Great and Good Friend
    I have received the letter which your majesty addressed to me
on 31 day of March last announcing the pleasing intelligence of
the marriage on the 10th of that month of Her Majesty's dearly
beloved Son His Royal Highness Albert Edward, Prince of Wales, Duke
of Surrey, Prince of Saxe-Coburg and Gotha etc etc with Her Royal
Highness, the Princess Alexandra Caroline Maria Charlotte Lovita
Julia, eldest daughter of His Royal Highness the Prince Christian of
Denmark. Feeling a lively interest in whatever concerns the welfare
and happiness of Your Majesty's illustrious House, I pray Your
Majesty to receive my cordial congratulations on this auspicious
event, and my fervent wishes that it may signally promote your own
happiness and that of the Prince, your son and his young spouse And
to recommend Your Majesty and Your Majesty's Royal Family to the
protection of the Almighty.
    Written at Washington the 18th day of May, in the year of our
Lord one Thousand eight hundred and sixty three

                            Your Good Friend

                            Abraham Lincoln

By the President
            William H Sevard
                    Secretary of State

THE NEXT DANCE!

Lord Punch. "NOW, MY BOY! THERE'S YOUR PRETTY COUSIN COLUMBIA—YOU DON'T GET SUCH A PARTNER AS THAT EVERY DAY!"

This *Punch* cartoon shows a youthful Prince on his North American tour of 1860. He is being introduced as a dancing partner to Columbia, depicted as a beautiful young woman in a dress dotted with the stars of her nation's flag.

An 'extremely critical position'
General Charles Gordon to Major General Redvers Buller

14 DECEMBER 1884

This document is a letter from General Charles Gordon to Major General Redvers Buller, the chief-of-staff of the Sudan Expeditionary Force, better known as the Nile Expedition. Dated 14 December 1884, it expresses Gordon's desperate need for reinforcements as he was besieged in Khartoum.

Gordon's story combines all the necessary elements to turn it into a myth: besieged in the hostile capital city of a no-less-hostile far-off land, repelling repeated attacks from 'savages', his situation could only fuel the imperialist imagination of his contemporaries.

The Mahdist Revolt, a religious uprising led by Muhammad Ahmad bin Abd Allah, self-proclaimed redeemer of the Islamic faith, had broken out in the Sudan before the British invasion of Egypt in 1882. By the summer of 1883, most British residents in Cairo considered the Sudan a lost cause – and one rather devoid of interest. However, the Egyptian ruler, Khedive Tewfik Pasha, thought otherwise and decided Colonel William Hicks and 10,000 men should head south and reconquer the Sudan, which was still nominally an Egyptian province. As a result, on 8 September 1883, Hicks's mission was wiped out by the Mahdist troops.

General Charles Gordon.

In January 1884 it was decided that Gordon should proceed to Cairo and report to Lord Cromer, the British agent and consul general. In Cairo, Gordon met with the Khedive. Tewfik then issued two decrees. The first one was Gordon's appointment as governor general of the Sudan, and the second contained his orders: evacuate the Egyptian garrisons and establish a Sudanese government headed by tribal leaders to administrate those territories that hadn't fallen into the hands of the Mahdists.

On 26 January 1884, Gordon left for the Sudan, accompanied by Lieutenant Colonel Stewart who, he complained, was sent 'to be his wet nurse'. They arrived in Khartoum on 18 February 1884. The city was isolated, but the situation wasn't hopeless yet as there were still substantial quantities of food, water and ammunition.

The siege, which was to last 317 days, began on 13 March. Gordon, who had been described by Cromer as 'terribly flighty', could also be awfully stubborn. He decided to stay and fight. Although everything indicated that London had no intention of helping,

Gordon never ceased to call for reinforcements and to wait for them to come, galvanising his troops by announcing the imminent arrival of British detachments at regular intervals.

In Britain, voices started being raised, demanding that an expedition should be sent to relieve Gordon. Under tremendous pressure from the press, the public opinion and even Queen Victoria, Prime Minister Gladstone, who had been staunchly opposed to a relief expedition, finally relented. General Wolseley, who had successfully invaded Egypt in 1882, thus left Cairo for Khartoum on 27 September 1884. By then, Gordon's situation was truly desperate, and he wrote in his diary that it would soon be 'too late'.

The first British troops reached Khartoum on 28 January 1885. Unusually, the Egyptian colours were not flying over the palace. Gordon had been right – it was too late. The city had fallen in the early hours of 26 January, the garrison and the inhabitants had been massacred, and Gordon himself had been killed and beheaded.

The telegram Gordon had sent to the governor of Khartoum in January 1884, saying: 'Don't be in a funk. You are men, not women. I am coming. Tell the inhabitants' shows that Gordon had a slightly exaggerated sense of his own importance and power. He did, however, capture the imagination of his contemporaries and when his death was announced on 5 February 1885 the whole British nation raised against Gladstone, whom they held responsible and who, in the space of a night, saw his nickname change from GOM ('grand old man') to MOG ('murderer of Gordon'). No doubt Gordon would have appreciated this, even though he states in this letter dated 14 December 1884 that he didn't have 'any feeling of bitterness to Her Majesty's Government', and was describing his desperate situation 'merely as a matter of fact'.

In the words of Kitchener, who was to lead another (more successful) expedition to the Sudan in 1898: 'never was a garrison so nearly rescued, never was a commander so lamented.'

Copy.

Kartoum

14. 12. 84

Sir

I send down the steamer "Bordeen" tomorrow with Vol VI of my private Journal containing account of the events in Kartoum from 5 Nov to 14 Decr. The state of affairs is such that one cannot foresee further than 5 to 7 days, after which the town may at any time, fall. I have done all, in my power to hold out, but I own, I consider the position is extremely critical almost desperate, & I say this, without any feeling of bitterness, with respect to H. M. Govt., but merely as a matter of fact. Should the town fall; it will be questionable whether it will be worth the while of H. M. X̶X̶X̶ G̶y̶. to continue its expedition, for it is certain, that the fall of Kartoum will insure that of Kasala & Sennaar.

I have &c.

(sd) C. G. Gordon.

The Chief of Staff
Soudan Expdy Force

Khartoum

14.12.84

Sir,

     I send down the steamer "Berdeen" to-morrow
with Vol. VI. of my private journal, containing
account of the events in Khartoum from 5th November
to 14th December. The state of affairs is such
that one cannot foresee further than five to seven
days, after which the town may at any time fall.
I have done all in my power to hold out, but I
own I consider the position is extremely critical,
almost desperate; and I say this without any feeling
of bitterness to Her Majesty's Government, but
merely as a matter of fact. Should the town fall,
it will be questionable whether it will be worth
the while of Her Majesty's Government to continue
its expedition; for it is certain that the fall of
Khartoum will insure that of Kasala and Sennaar.

I have, &c.

Sir

C. G. Gordon

The Chief of Staff
  Sudan Expeditionary Force

Bravery in Belgium
Words of warning to the mother of Edith Cavell

At the point that the First World War was declared in the summer of 1914, Edith Cavell was on holiday at home near Norwich. Upon hearing the news, she immediately made moves to return to the medical establishment she had helped to set up in 1907. Situated just outside Brussels, this had been the first training college for lay nurses of its type in Belgium. Now, in the autumn of 1914, the school became a Red Cross Hospital, treating German and Belgian soldiers alike. However, when Brussels fell to the Germans the majority of the British nurses were sent home. Not so Edith and her assistant, who remained, continuing to nurse the wounded and sick.

Among the collections held at The National Archives is a file containing correspondence pertaining to Edith. This includes a letter that was written by the Countess of Borchgrave on the instructions of her husband, travelled from Belgium, then was passed from one chief constable via the Ministry of Information to another chief constable, before it was finally delivered to Edith's mother. Within the three weeks it took for the letter to make its way to Norwich, Edith had been arrested by the German authorities. It was not initially clear who might have betrayed her, at least to the British authorities. What we do know is that the warnings contained therein, that Mrs Cavell should not speak of her daughter's whereabouts to anyone, came too late: Edith had been arrested in Brussels on 5 August. By the time her mother received the letter Edith was in solitary confinement, as she would remain until her execution.

During her imprisonment, Edith confessed to having harboured British and French soldiers in her house, in addition to Belgians of military ages, and to facilitating their escape to neutral territory.

In consequence, Cavell was tried in a closed court and sentenced to death on 11 October 1915, and executed at 2am the following day – an act that caused shock and outrage throughout the world. While it was broadly acknowledged that the sentence for such actions under German military law was death, the execution of a woman who worked only to save lives, including those of German soldiers earlier in the war, was widely condemned, as was the swift fulfilment of her sentence. Both Spanish and American authorities had tried to intervene in the case but the hasty turnaround between sentence and commutation had rendered their efforts useless.

Edith Cavell.

The execution of Edith Cavell led to some discussion among the British authorities about whether this should not make the case for carrying out death sentences passed on women found guilty of German espionage in Britain. The outcry against what was considered by some as a breach of the Geneva Conventions spread across the country, and the case was covered extensively in the British press.

A hundred years on, the extent to which Edith may or may not have acted in any way beyond purely humanitarian ones remains unclear. We do know, however, that in 1919 a man by the name of Quien was put on trial and convicted in France for his part in the betrayal to the Germans of Edith Cavell's organisation – which had been established to help Allied servicemen to escape from Occupied France and Belgium to the safety of Holland.

In addition to correspondence between government officials concerning Cavell's case, the file also contains photographs of her grave and place of execution, which were sent by the French authorities to the Security Service for forwarding to her mother in 1917. After the end of the First World War, Cavell's body was repatriated from Belgium in 1919 and she received a state funeral. In addition to her grave in Norwich Cathedral, Cavell is commemorated by a memorial in St Martin's Place, London, which was unveiled in 1920.

BERKSHIRE CONSTABULARY.

40535

TELEPHONE NO.   11.

REF. NO.   213/15.

SUPERINTENDENT'S OFFICE,

COUNTY POLICE STATION,

Wokingham

1st August   191 5.

[stamp: BERKSHIRE CONSTABULARY / CHIEF CONSTABLE'S OFFICE / 2 Aug 1915 / COUNTY POLICE STATION, / READING.]

Sir,

I beg to report that today I saw the Countess Camille
de Borchgrave, at Brougham House, Crowthorne, with reference
to the letter sent to The Chief Constable of Reading, enclosing
letter addressed to Mrs Cavell 24 Col Road Norwich, and asking
that it be sent through The Chief Constable, Norwich.
The Countess states that her Husband is in Brussels, and he had
written to say that it is extremely dangerous for a English
Woman to be within the Country occupied by the German Army, and
she The Countess was to caution Mrs Cavell that her daughter
[handwritten: Decoded 23.8.1]
(who is a Nurse left in Brussels) is alright now, but if she
talks to people about her, it may get known to the Germans, and
if it does there is no telling what might be her fate. The man
who she describes in her letter is believed to be a German spy
trying to obtain the address of Miss Cavell in Brussels.
Count Borchgrave told his Wife she was to at once send to Mrs
Cavell through the Police.

I am Sir,
Your Obedient Servant,
[signature: Chas Goddard]
Superintendent.

The Chief Constable,
of Berkshire,
Reading.

POST OFFICE TELEGRAPHS.

Office Stamp.

Office of Origin and Service Instructions.

Enfield

Charges to pay

s. d.
15 150

Handed in at 10.55 .M.,

Received here at 11.25 .M.

16 OCT 1915

TO { Foreign Office Lon

Urgent wire truth report of
Miss Cavell murdered in Brussels
Also fate of Companions
Mallory Claysmore Enfield

To: Foreign Office

Urgent wire with report of

Miss Cavell murdered in Brussels

Also fate of Companions

Malloy Claysmore Enfield

Keeping schtum
Letter to Churchill regarding the *Ultra* secret

24 JUNE 1941

The German high command entered the Second World War in the belief that its military communications were unbreakable. To encode their messages, the Germans relied on the use of the Enigma machine, developed in the 1920s by Arthur Scherbius, an electrical engineer. This resembled a typewriter, with each letter connected to an illuminated display board via a system of electromechanical rotors that rotated every time a key was pressed. To add further complexity, the rotors were connected to a plug board on the front of the machine where pairs of letters were transposed. To decode the message, the operator needed to know the exact settings of the rotors and cables on the original machine. As these settings were changed on a daily basis, the task of intercepting the message and deciphering it was believed to be impossible.

This confidence was misplaced. Unknown to the Germans, the Polish Cipher Bureau had managed to obtain a commercial version of the Enigma machine and by 1933 had devised a method that enabled them to read German radio messages enciphered using Enigma. With war imminent, the Poles decided to share their secrets with British intelligence. The information was passed to the Government Code and Cipher School, which during the war was located at Bletchley Park in Buckinghamshire.

The Germans were convinced that messages sent using Enigma could not be broken and it was therefore used for communications on the battlefield, at sea and in the air. The British described any intelligence gained from Enigma as 'Ultra', and considered it top secret. To safeguard the source and prevent the Germans from realising their codes had been broken, British intelligence created a fictional spy called Boniface, who controlled a series of well-placed agents throughout Germany. In fact Boniface was the code name used as a cover name for Ultra; only a select few commanders were made aware of the full significance of Ultra, and use of the term was used sparingly to maintain confidentiality.

The security implications presented by Ultra meant that intelligence gathered by Bletchley Park could not be shared with the Americans or Russians without potentially compromising the source. The British prime minister, Winston Churchill, was informed of the situation in a letter written in June 1941 by Sir Stewart Menzies, the chief of the Secret Intelligence Service (MI6). In the letter, Menzies warns Churchill against divulging the Ultra secret to President Roosevelt as there was no safe means of disguising the source 'should there be any indiscretion in the USA'. The prospect of sharing intelligence with the Russians was no better. It was known that Russian military ciphers were compromised and that 'it would only be a matter of days before the Germans would know of our success' and adopt new ciphers – thus depriving Britain of a vital source of intelligence. Menzies signed the letter with a 'C' in green ink, a tradition continued in the service to this day.

Churchill accepted that no such risks should be taken and informed Menzies that he should act to ensure that Ultra intelligence remained tightly controlled. The existence of Ultra was finally revealed in 1974 with the publication of *The Ultra Secret* by FW Winterbottom, an RAF officer who supervised the distribution of Ultra intelligence.

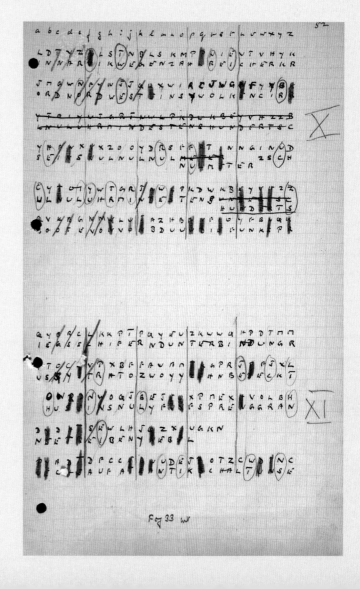

The mathematical theory behind the Enigma machine, devised by Alan Turing.

MOST SECRET

C/6863.

LONDON,

24th June, 1941.

PRIME MINISTER.

After considering, from all angles, the
possibility of divulging to the President the information
regarding U.S. Naval Units being chased by U. Boats, I
find myself unable to devise any safe means of wrapping
up the information in a manner which would not imperil
this source, which should, without fail, play a vital part
in the Battle of the Atlantic.

The fact that the message in question was passed
by the Admiral Commanding U. Boats to submarines actually
operating, renders it well nigh impossible that the information
could have been secured by an agent, and however much we
insist that it came from a highly placed source, I greatly
doubt the enemy being for a moment deceived, should there be
any indiscretion in the U.S.A. That this might occur, cannot
be ruled out, as the Americans are not in any sense as
security minded as one would wish, and I need only draw your
attention to the attached cutting from to-day's "Daily Express",
on a matter which, in my opinion, should not have been made
public if the two Secret Services are to work together as
closely as is imperative.

It is true that the American experts who visited
the United Kingdom gave us a very valuable insight into
Japanese cryptographic methods, but they, themselves, impressed
upon me how cautious they were in passing any of the results
to the State Department.

At a recent Meeting of the Chiefs of Staff, it was
agreed that information derived from this Most Secret source
should only be communicated to the U.S. Naval and Military
Authorities when we were satisfied that the source was not
endangered. I believe that any other decision as regards
weakening the veil of secrecy would cause the greatest regret
at a later date, and I similarly hold the view that it would
be fatal to divulge to the Russians immediate information
which we are securing about German operational intentions on
the Eastern Front. To be of any value, it would mean that the
information would be immediately transmitted to the Commanders

in/

in the Field, and as the Russian Military cyphers are
compromised, it would only be a matter of days before
the Germans would know of our success, and operations
in the future would almost certainly be hidden in an
unbreakable way.

C

Certainly have no such risks as A

Have you acted in this sense? If not
do so.

24. VI

Certainly have no such risks as A

Have you acted in this sense? If not
do so.

Restrained words to a disgraced president
Harold Wilson's letter of thanks to Richard Nixon

9 AUGUST 1974

On 8 August 1974, the 37th President of the USA Richard Nixon addressed the American nation from the Oval Office of the White House and announced his resignation; to date, the only serving president to resign from office in US history.

His action was the culmination of the Watergate scandal that had dominated Washington politics during the early 1970s. The affair began on the night of 17 June 1972 with the arrest of five men who were attempting to break into the offices of the Democratic National Committee at the Watergate hotel and office complex. The purpose of the break-in was to plant listening devices in the office phones, with one of the men claiming to have worked for the CIA. In the subsequent FBI investigation it was discovered that a cheque for $25,000 that had been earmarked for the Nixon campaign was being held in the bank account of one of those arrested. The cash was linked to a slush fund used by the Committee for the Re-Election of the President (CREEP), the organisation responsible for running Nixon's 1972 election campaign.

In a series of articles published in the *Washington Post* it became apparent that the burglary was connected to the Nixon White House. Testimony provided by former staff members of the administration revealed that Nixon had installed a tape-recording system in his office and had recorded numerous conversations. The Senate Watergate Committee that had been established to investigate the affair demanded copies of the tapes: Nixon refused and disconnected the recording system. In an attempt to halt the

Richard Nixon.

investigation, Nixon fired the special prosecutor, Archibald Cox, and agreed to hand over some of the tapes. It was too late. In July the Supreme Court ordered Nixon to turn over the remaining tapes and voted to impeach the president for obstruction of justice and abuse of power. The tapes were eventually released on 5 August and showed that Nixon had been informed of the break-in soon after it had occurred and had approved plans to obstruct the investigation. His impeachment by the Senate almost certain, he resigned from office on 8 August 1974.

The resignation of Nixon placed the British prime minister, Harold Wilson, in a difficult position. Unable to support President Nixon personally, he was nevertheless anxious to maintain the strong Anglo-American relationship between the two countries. Writing to Nixon on 9 August 1974, Wilson praised him for putting the interests of the USA before his own personal considerations and offered his sympathy for the anguish that Nixon and his family were facing. Wilson concluded his short letter by thanking Nixon for his continuing efforts for world peace and his contribution to the Western alliance.

Nixon died on 27 April 1994 and was given a state funeral attended by Presidents Clinton, Ford, Carter, Reagan and Bush. The term Watergate has now become a byword for any political scandal involving the abuse of power and attempted cover-up.

Registry
No.

personal

DRAFT / message

Type 1 +

SECURITY CLASSIFICATION

To:- Mr Nixon

FROM

Prime Minister
Telephone No. Ext.

Department

Top Secret.
Secret.
Confidential.
Restricted.
Unclassified.

PRIVACY MARKING

.... In Confidence

*There is a
widespread
understanding
in Britain of
~~Political~~
~~leaders everywhere~~
~~will nations~~
~~will understand~~
the courage
which your
decision required
of you, and
which you
brought to it.*

I have just learned the news of your
resignation from the Presidency of the
United States. I ~~well~~ realise the anguish
with which you must have reached this
momentous decision, which is of such
significance for your country, your family
and yourself. ~~It is not for me to comment
in any way the~~ [domestic] ~~reasons which
have led to this decision.~~ ~~But~~ I would
~~none the less~~ like you to know how greatly
I have valued your contribution to the
cause of world peace, to the Western Alliance
and to relationship between our two countries.
*And I was moved to see and hear
you last night dedicate your
continuing efforts to these causes,
for which you have done so much in
your presidency.*

*May I send you my best
personal wishes to you and your
family.*

NOTHING TO BE WRITTEN IN THIS MARGIN

(3002) Dmd. 145244 400M 10/73 LLtd. 839/1

First insert: There is a widespread understanding
                in Britain of the courage which
                your decision required of you, and
                which you brought to it.

Second insert: And I was moved to see and hear you
                last night dedicate your continuing
                efforts to these causes, for which
                you have done so much in your
                presidency.
                        May I send you my best
                personal wishes to you and your
                family.

A brother's desperate quest for information
Letter from Noor Khan's brother, Vilayat Khan

16 JULY 1947

Noor Inayat Khan was born in Russia but spent most of her childhood in Paris. Her mother was American and her father was an Indian mystic teacher who descended from the last Mogul emperor of southern India. After France fell to the Nazis, Noor escaped to England and worked in the Women's Auxiliary Air Force (WAAF) as a wireless operator. From here, she was recruited by the Special Operations Executive (SOE) in 1942.

Set up by the government to train and operate secret agents for missions in enemy territory, the SOE provided vital support for the war effort. Noor was the first female wireless operator to be sent to Nazi-occupied France during the Second World War. Her mission document sets out details about her role: she was to maintain a link between the circuit in the field and London by receiving messages about planned sabotage operations and where arms were needed to support the resistance. This was an extremely dangerous job that required Noor to find a secure place from which to transmit. If she needed to move location she had to transport her bulky transmitter with her, which made her highly vulnerable to detection.

Four months after Noor's arrival in France she was betrayed by Renée Garry, a French woman who was allegedly in love with another SOE agent named France Antelme. Garry felt spurned by Antelme and perceived a love triangle in which Antelme was transferring his affection to Noor. Betrayed for revenge, Noor was captured by the Gestapo. She was initially held in the Gestapo prison on Avenue Foch in Paris, from where she attempted to escape on two separate occasions, before being sent to Pforzheim Prison in November 1943. Here, Noor was kept in solitary confinement and subjected to repeated beatings and torture. Despite this, she refused to give away any information and after ten months was transferred to Dachau concentration camp. On 13 September 1944, Noor was shot and killed, although different accounts of Noor's story give 11 or 12 September as dates of her execution.

Born in Russia, raised in France and of mixed US and Indian blood, Noor Inayat Khan nevertheless acted with incredible bravery to further the British cause during the Second World War.

In this letter, knowledge about Noor's death is not yet known. Vilayat writes asking for information about where his sister could be. Although he says that he has given up hope of ever seeing his sister again, there is an underlying thread of possibility that maybe she might still be alive. He writes about the detainment camps and whether it could just be possible that she is still being held *'I don't suppose that there is any chance...'* even though *'I understand that all of the British have been retrieved...'*

Vilayat also seeks to pursue other avenues that had previously been denied to him, asking if he can now make enquiries through the Red Cross and whether the security grounds that had prevented this line of enquiry, still apply. His desperate need to find out what has really happened to his sister is thinly veiled in this letter; the way in which Noor's disappearance and the complete absence of information about her fate has ripped a hole in their lives, conveyed by his final sentences *'Is it not possible at this stage to know something of the circumstances of her capture and the work she was doing?'*

Noor's tragic fate; her imprisonment and subsequent execution, were not fully confirmed to her Vilayat and the rest of Noor's family until 1947. She had been mentioned in dispatches in 1946 as she was still considered 'missing' at that stage. In 1949, Noor Khan was posthumously awarded the George Cross for outstanding bravery.

HM ML 206
c/o G.P.O. London

July 16th '46

To F.O. Atkins.

Dear Madam,

I must apologise for worrying you
again for news of my sister, but so much time has now passed
since the time of the collapse of Germany that I have lost in
my own mind any hope of ever seeing my sister again.
But surely, is there so far no clue at all as to her last whereabouts?
I don't suppose there is any chance that she should still be in
a D.P. camp, since I understand that all the British
have been retrieved.

I had been asked by Maj. McKenzie not to make
any enquiries through the Red Cross on security grounds;
does this still apply?

Is it not possible at this stage to know something
of the circumstances of her capture & the work she was
doing?

Yours sincerely,
Sub-Lt. R.N.V.R.

HMML 206

c/o G.P.O. London

July 16th '45

To F.O. Atkins

        Dear Madam

                I must apologise for worrying you
again for news of my sister, but too much time has now
passed since the time of the collapse of Germany that
I have lost in my own mind any hope of ever seeing my
sister again. But surely, is there so far no clue at
all as to her last whereabouts? I don't suppose there
is any chance that she should still be in a D.P camp,
since I understand that all the British have been
retrieved.

        I had been asked by Maj Mackenzie not to make my
enquiries through the Red Cross on security grounds;
does this still apply?

        Is it not possible at this stage to know
something of the circumstances of her capture and the
work she was doing?

        Yours sincerely

                Vilayat Sub Lieut R.N.V.R.

Scoring points with potatoes
Raisa Gorbacheva's potato recipe letter

19 JULY 1985

The mid-1980s was a time of ratcheting Cold War tensions: of the 'evil empire'; Operation Able Archer; Olympic Games' boycotts; and the ever-present fear of mutually assured destruction. However, while news of Ronald Reagan's 'Star Wars' project was dominating the airwaves, wags at the British Ministry for Agriculture, Fisheries and Food may have been forgiven for thinking of UK-Soviet relations in the context of 'Spudnik'.

Mikhail Gorbachev became Soviet premier in March 1985. Prior to this, in the previous December, he had led a parliamentary delegation to the UK during which a cautiously optimistic Prime Minister Margaret Thatcher found him a man with whom she could do business. The Soviet delegation was hosted at the prime minister's country retreat, Chequers, a sixteenth-century manor house set at the foot of the Chiltern Hills in a green corner of Buckinghamshire, forty miles north-west of London.

Raisa Gorbachev.

During lunch one day, Gorbachev's wife, Raisa – a lecturer at Moscow State University – apparently became engaged in conversation about potato recipes with the British government Minister for Agriculture, Fisheries and Food, Michael Jopling. The conversation clearly stuck with Mrs Gorbacheva as she wrote to Jopling months later recalling his somewhat attitude to her insistence that there were three hundred Byelorussian recipes for the humble potato. Determined to prove this to be the case, she vowed to send Jopling evidence in the form of a cookery book on her return to Moscow.

This she did, although in her letter the Soviet first lady had to confess an error, writing: 'My apologies for being somewhat inaccurate, in fact there are *five hundred*, rather than three hundred, recipes to cook potatoes.' A cookery book was also dispatched to Whitehall. Some weeks later, Ivor Llewelyn, at the Ministry for Agriculture, Fisheries and Food, wrote to his Foreign and Commonwealth Office colleague Len Appleyard to triumphantly declare: 'We have the book … it is in Russian.' Llewelyn continued, offering: 'If you have anyone who reads Russian and has a fondness for potatoes, we would be happy to lend it.' The correspondence even caught the attention of Margaret Thatcher as her private secretary, Charles Powell, noted: 'Prime Minister. Fascinating evidence of a new style!' Sadly, the official record doesn't reveal whether anybody accepted the offer to borrow the cookery book. However, it is no longer with the original file so perhaps a willing taker with a fondness for potatoes and a proficiency in Russian was indeed found!

Mr. Michael JOPLING,
Minister of Agriculture
of Great Britain

July 19, 1985

Esteemed Mr. Jopling,

When the Soviet parliamentary delegation headed by
Mikhail S.Gorbachev was on a visit to your country, I told
you at the luncheon at Chequers that in Byelorussia we have
three hundred recipes to cook potatoes. It seemed to me that
you were doubtful about it and I promised to send you a book
containing information in this regard at a later date.

I am keeping my promise. My apologies for being somewhat
inaccurate: in fact, there are five hundred, rather than three
hundred, recipes to cook potatoes.

I avail myself of this opportunity to express once again
appreciation for the attention and welcome accorded to us in
Britain. We remember all the talks and meetings, and the
atmosphere in which they were held. One would like to believe
that all this will promote mutual understanding, confidence
and co-operation between the peoples of our two countries.

With best wishes

Raisa GORBACHEVA

'Overcoming the division of our continent'
Margaret Thatcher's letter of congratulations to Helmut Kohl

3 OCTOBER 1990

This document is a short letter Margaret Thatcher sent Helmut Kohl, the German Chancellor, on 3 October 1990 – the day of the German reunification. In it she writes: 'The unification of Germany represents an important step in overcoming the division of our continent', but in reality Margaret Thatcher hadn't always been that enthusiastic about a united Germany.

Helmut Kohl.

The situation in East Germany (the German Democratic Republic, or GDR) had only really appeared on the agenda of Cabinet meetings in September 1989; since the borders had been opened between Hungary and Austria, more and more people were fleeing the GDR, and there were demonstrations in large cities such as Dresden and Leipzig. This marked the beginning of what was called the 'peaceful revolution', which culminated on 4 November when half a million people gathered on the Alexanderplatz in Berlin to demand change. On 7 November, the East German Council of Ministers resigned, followed by the whole Politburo a day later. The British government knew the situation was extremely volatile, but they were convinced that most East Germans were calling for reforms within East Germany rather than unification with West Germany. When the Berlin Wall fell on the evening of 9 November 1989 it therefore came somewhat as a surprise. On the following day, Margaret Thatcher talked to Helmut Kohl on the phone. She had been watching the events in Berlin and thought 'they were some of the most historic she had ever seen'.

From then on, things moved very quickly – too quickly for Thatcher, who welcomed the opportunity for greater freedom and deeper reforms but thought structure was of the utmost importance. For her, the only way to avoid the collapse of the NATO front line and of Gorbachev's hopes for reform was to use the existing Four-Power structure. The 1971 Quadripartite Agreement on Berlin had reaffirmed the rights and responsibilities of Britain, France, the Soviet Union and the USA in Germany as a whole, and Margaret Thatcher was a staunch believer in its principles. She therefore pushed for 2+4 meetings (attended by the two Germanys and the four Allied powers) and more consultation.

Thatcher's relations with Kohl, it must be said, were notoriously bad. Kohl's ten-point speech at the Bundestag, the German parliament, on 28 November 1989 didn't help.

He declared that reunification remained the objective of the federal government and that the two Germanys would proceed towards unity. Thatcher thought this was somewhat premature, and was furious that he hadn't consulted the Allies first.

At the end of January 1990, Gorbachev shifted his position from outright opposition to the reunification to stating that no one was placing the principle of German reunification in doubt. Thatcher, however, remained unconvinced and had a long list of concerns. She thought Kohl wanted reunification at any cost, despite the political consequences it could have; she was worried it might lead to a socialist government in Germany; and she was concerned a reunified Germany would exercise too much power in Europe. Finally, she also thought 'Germany had a tendency to forget that the division of Germany was the result of a war which Germany had started'. In February 1990, Douglas Hurd, the foreign secretary, warned: 'we must not appear to be a brake on everything.'

In the spirit of consultation, a seminar was held at Chequers on 24 March 1990. Questions covered included 'who are the Germans?' (the answer wasn't very flattering, as attributes included 'angst, aggressiveness, assertiveness, bullying, egotism, inferiority complex, sentimentality'); 'have the Germans changed?' (attendants agreed that 'today's Germans were very different from their predecessors'); and 'will a united Germany aspire to dominate Eastern Europe?' Thatcher only wanted a thorough assessment of Germany, but her private secretary, Charles Powell, commented at the time: 'it would be very embarrassing and gravely damaging to our interests if the content of so frank a discussion of one of our closest allies were to become known.'

In the end, Thatcher had to come on board. She still wasn't convinced by the idea of a united Germany, but had become increasingly isolated in Europe and within her own Cabinet. At least, she thought, the 2+4 meetings she had insisted on had provided a solution to the external implications of German reunification.

Still, one can't help but wonder whether Helmut Kohl's reply to this 3 October letter might not have been slightly sarcastic: 'I should like to express my special gratitude for your personal support and the support of your Government on the way to German unity.'

10 DOWNING STREET

LONDON SW1A 2AA

THE PRIME MINISTER   3 October 1990

Dear Helmut-

I offer you my warmest congratulations on this special day
when your country is once again united. The unification of
Germany represents an important step in overcoming the division
of our continent. Together with our Allies, we withstood the
difficult period of the Cold War. Now Germany is to be united
in peace and freedom. A united Germany will have a profoundly
important role in Europe as we face the future as friends,
allies and partners.

Warm regards,

Yours ever

Margaret

His Excellency Dr. Helmut Kohl

Revellers on the Berlin Wall celebrate the fall of communism in East Germany.

Conflict, unrest
and protest

The vanquishing of the Armada
Sir Francis Drake's report on the Battle of Gravelines

SUMMER 1588

The Spanish Armada – fought between 29 July and 12 August (New Style; Old style by English reckoning 19 July– 2 August) – is one of the most famous events in English history. Not only did it ensure the survival of Elizabethan Protestant England but the victory was a milestone in the history of the Royal Navy, heralding its inexorable rise to the formidable instrument of British global power it would later become.

Had the Armada invasion of 1588 succeeded, it is debatable whether England would have suffered the humiliation of total annexation to the Spanish Empire. Nevertheless, Elizabeth would have most likely been deposed and England forcefully returned to the fold of the Catholic Church. At the very least the price of peace with Spain for Protestant England would have included agreement to end all military and financial aid to Dutch rebels in the Spanish Netherlands and attacks on Spanish ships and settlements by English privateers.

Though King Philip II of Spain was an intelligent and meticulous planner, some of his own subjects believed the king's 'enterprise of England' was a flawed endeavour from the outset. The delays and disruption to preparations caused by the lack of a centralised system of naval administration meant that any hopes of secrecy were quickly extinguished. Moreover, the Marquis of Santa Cruz, the Armada's commander until his death in February 1588, shared private concerns with fellow officer, Martin de Bertendona, about the lack of a deep-water port in Spanish hands in Flanders. This would have enabled Spanish forces being marshalled by the Duke of Parma to embark safely under escort from large Spanish warships. Parma in correspondence with Philip had even identified the port of Flushing as a secure and suitable port for embarkation if it could be successfully captured from Dutch rebels.

Such wise foresight was considered negligible or too inconvenient by Philip but would prove to be the critical flaw in the Armada plan. Once the Spanish fleet, commanded by the Duke of Medina Sidonia, had successfully sailed through the English Channel, larger Spanish vessels could not safely sail close to shore in the treacherous shallow waters around Dunkirk and Calais where Parma's army had assembled. Without their protection, Parma's army was highly vulnerable to attack by Dutch shallow draft vessels known as 'flyboats' patrolling close to Dunkirk.

Sir Francis Drake.

Nevertheless the Armada, with a total complement of over 19,000 soldiers and 8,500 sailors, posed a grave threat to Elizabethan England in its own right. The battle that took place off Gravelines on the Flemish coast on 8 August (New style; Old style 29 July) between English and Spanish fleets was the climax in naval operations during the armada episode and would prove crucially decisive. The English navy under the command of Admiral Lord Howard of Effingham had not succeeded in breaking the Armada's rigid defensive formation nor inflicted much damage to Spanish ships as the fleet made its way down the English Channel. New tactics it seemed would be required. On the night of 7 August (New Style; Old Style 28 July) several English fire ships were unleashed on the Spanish fleet laying at anchor near Calais and despite efforts to hold formation, the Armada scattered. The following morning English vessels with their superior firepower and manoeuvrability attacked, now daring to fire their broadsides at closer range to devastating effect. Two ships were sunk and two more driven onto the shoals whilst many others sustained serious damage. Sir Francis Drake in his letter to Sir Francis Walsingham celebrated that 'God hath geven us so good a day in forcing the enemy so far to leeward as I hope in god the prince of parma: and the duke of Sodonya shall not shake handes this fewe dayes.'

The Spanish fleet was now in mortal danger of being driven by winds onto the perilous sandbanks off Zeeland, though fortunately, the winds changed at the last minute allowing the fleet to escape northward. In requesting further munitions and victuals, Drake's letter showed that he believed their fight was far from over, a view shared by his fellow commanders. Unbeknown to them, Spanish morale had been fatally weakened and with dwindling supplies, prevailing northerly winds and the determined pursuit of the English fleet, any resolve to offer further defiance shattered. The Armada would thus limp home via the turbulent seas around Scotland and western Ireland. Though flawed Spanish planning and the turbulent weather played their part, ultimate acclaim should be reserved for Drake and fellow commanders and sailors of the Elizabethan navy in the victory against the might of the Spanish Empire.

Right ho[nourable] this bearer cam [came] a board
the ship I was in in a wonderfful good tyme and
brought with hym as good knowledge as we culd wyshe,
his carffulnes therin is worthy recompence for that
god hath geven us so good a day in forcying the
enemy so far to leeward as I hope in god the prince
of parma: and the duke of Sodonya shall not shake
handes this Fewe dayes, And when so ever they shall
meet. I beleve nether of them will greatly reioyce
of this dayes Servis the town of Callys [Calais]
hath seene sum p[ar]te thereof whose major yo[ur]
ma[jes]tie is beholding unto: businis comandes me to
end, god bless her ma[jes]tie our gracyous Sovraygne
and geve us all grace and leve in his feare,
I asure yo[ur] ho[nour] this dayes S[er]vis hath mych
[much] apald the enemy and no doubt but incoraged
ou[r] army from a board her ma[jes]ties good ship the
revenge this 29th July 1588 [Old Style; New Style,
8 August 1588]

        Yo[u]r ho[nour's] most redy to be co[m]manded

            Fra[ncis] Drake

Yo[u]rs Fra[ncis] Drake.
...ther must be great care taken to send us whether so ever
the enemy goeth monycyon [munition] and vittual [victual].

Home front anguish during the English Civil War
An unknown woman speaks out about suffering

The English Civil War lasted nearly a decade and had a devastating impact on Britain on both a personal and political level: rifts were created in families that took generations to heal, and seven per cent of the population died as a direct result of the fighting or the famine or disease that arose in the wake of the war. For women on both sides of the conflict the effect on their lives was immense. Often they were the ones left trying to hold families together or to maintain households deprived of financial support. They lost husbands, sons or homes or were driven into exile. This fragment of a letter from an unknown woman on the Parliamentary side provides an insight into the privations suffered and the upset felt in both camps.

The writer herself describes it as a distressed letter and it conveys an immediate uncensored anguish: her feelings tumble out in a stream of consciousness unfettered by punctuation. She tells of the financial burden experienced by families struggling to support husbands and sons shifted from garrison to garrison and of the suffering and uncertainty felt by families who often did not know where their soldiers were or even if they were still alive. She appeals for peace but consigns herself to her God. She is devout, patriotic and ready to die for her country but also resents the burdens placed upon herself and her family.

This letter has lain among the State Papers for nearly 400 years. We have no way of knowing whether the writer's plea was heard or what happened to her. Her emotions, however, cut through the centuries and convey a sense of immediacy to the reader. Like all the best letters, it provides an insight into an individual's state of mind and can add a personal dimension to a national conflict.

Another woman from the period, Margaret Eure, wrote 'in my poor judgement these times can bring no good end to them, that all women can do is pray for better for sure it is an ill time'. This letter is one such prayer.

Oliver Cromwell.

THE

KINGDOMES

weekly *Post*, with his packet of Letters,

publishing his meſſage to the City and Country,
this preſent *December* 28. 1643.

Arundel-caſtle	*His Excellency.*
Toceſter.	*Earl. Mancheſter.*
Oxford.	*Earle Newcaſtle.*
Turkie.	*Sir Willia. Waller.*
Poole.	*Sir Tho. Fairfax.*
York-ſhire.	*Sir Wil. Brereton.*
Lincoln-ſhire.	*Sir Jo. Meldrum.*
Flanders.	*S. Major Skippon.*
Scotland.	*Lord Hopton.*
Nampt wich.	*Recorder Derby.*
Cheſter.	*Mr. Hendersham.*
Grafton.	*Prince Rupert.*
Northumberland	*Lord Craford.*

1. The laſt newes from *Arundel* and of the true paſſages there.
2. Divers ſeverall victories latley obtained in the *North*, with the names of the Commanders, and the particulars of the ammunition ſurpriſed.
3. *Nuport* punnell being made good by ſupply from the Earle of *Mancheſter*, his Excellencyes deſigne from thence, and the reaſons thereof.
4. The plot in bringing over *Colonell* Munks Regiment from *Ireland* diſcovered.
5. An Example for a perpetuall warning peice for all. *Malignants* from *Dartmouth*.
6. Some plots diſcovered in the *North* and prevented.
7. With many other paſſages of great concernement.

Wedneſday. December 20.

THere were this day Letters out of *Dorſet-ſhire* certifying us, that the Cavaliers were plundring neere *Warham*, and had laden certaine Carts and Waggons with their pillage, wherewith they had an intent to have refreſht their quarters this Chriſtmas but a party of the Parliaments Forces which were marching betwixt *Poole* and *Warham*, having notice that the enemy was ſo nigh, marched upon them, and have taken their plunder from them, beſides ſome traine of ammunition,

C

and

my son of Andeuer time of stam hear
this due ant, which sir Thomas farfaxe
gaue him at bristo and upon a great
feet of the stone that he has had has forsed him to desier farfaxe to prelaunge
his time, well he haue tou ken som fisike
w'hich he has great nide of, next, his de
sier is if he could precuer it, to stae
hear, for after suche usege only for
my lo: Digebes pleasur, he is grone neue
werie of, and am I for his sake, to
sehawe he has bin fane to shifte from
garison to garison this somer, and the
cost it has put me to; so muche miser
then I could telle hawe to incompase
but al wee can doe I fear can not
gette them to parmite him to continue
hear exsept he agear befor them at lon
den; which he is neurie lothe to doe
althoe I beliue his pesse w'ill not be dificult to be made; What stikes w'the
him is as it mae conserne you, which
trust me he is fulle of consideration
of and so am I, nther was it sholl
be concluded of quickly for I am as

can not but hope a generall peace is at hand; es em ui
as some be to haue it so, but all the reason is le
me tell me it must be so, and I trust you ar
that nimble; althoe I wonder under fauer the
no niger talke of it in this partes that it hs
a thinge desired by your master and thos chu
him, and befor this that som thinge had bin do
but I fear to mame as a gainst this blesing
had wee ame thinge to chuse of, in this au
tractions it maught be disputed; but I thynk
that past time a clae after so muche ille
sukses; it tis not feet for me to sae anie
moer, but prae for peace and to be conten
withe suche a one as wee can gette, submit
my self to the almitie, and beliue this claes c
not haue bin but by Gods suffering all an
childer in ae hear but Thoms and Harrie the
haue written to you the rest present the
seruise to you, and I haue cause to dor
amonkst them God helpe me that I mae h
them; wile left his best sute withe you wh
he cam a wae I prae you let it be safe laed u
whefl he can hiue it, I will prae for you e
naly, desirin upon my knies to se you a ga

the 17 of october   I haue hear inclosed
                         letter was sent me of t
                         opinions at oxseferd

sir Thomas farfaxe gaue him at bristo and upon a great
feet of the stone that he has had has forsed him to
desier farfaxse to prelaunge his time, whell he haue
touken som fisike which he has great nide of; next, his
desier is if he could precuer it, to stae hear, for
after suche usege only for my Lo: Digebes pleasur, he
is grone uerie werie of, and so am I, for his sake,
to se hawe he has bin fane to shifte from garison to
garison this somer, and the cost it has put me to; so
muche moer then I could telle hawe to incompase but
all wee can doe I fear can not gette them to parmite
him to continue hear exsept he apear befor them at
londen, which he is uerrie lothe to doe althoe I
beliue his pesse will not be dificult to be made; What
stikes withe him is as it mae conserne you, which
trust me he is fulle of consideration of and so am I,
uther was it shold be concluded of qwikly for I am as
wearie of thos that haue bin his enimis as he, and I
beliue so is the publike which is worst of all; I

as som be to haue it so, but all the reason is left
me tels me it must be so, and I trust you ar of
that minde; althoe I wonder under fauer I hear no
moer talke of it in this partes that it tis a thinge
desired by your master and thos about him, and befor
this that som thinge had bin don but I fear to manie
ar against this blesinge had wee anie thinge to chuse
of, in this distractions it maught be disputed; but
I thinke that past time a dae after so muche ille
sukses; it tis not feet for me to sae anie moer, but
prae for pease and to be content with suche a one
as wee can gette, submiten my self to the almitie,
and beliue this daes cold not haue bin but by Gods
suffering all awe childerin ar hear but Thom; and
Harrie haue written to you the rest present ther
seruise to you, and I haue enufe to doe amonkst them
God helpe me that I mae help them, wille left his best
sute with you when he cam awae I prae you let it be
safe laed up whell he can haue it, I will prae for you
et[er]nally, desirin upon my knies to se you a gan

I haue hear inclosed a Letter was sent me of
the opinions at oxseferd

the 17 of october

Endorsed: 17 Octob 1645 I beleeue this letter
came from the Ladie of Barkshire

Political plea for a privateer
Despatch from General George Washington to Sir Guy Carleton

24 DECEMBER 1782

This document sent from the American Continental Army's headquarters at Newburgh (on the Hudson River) to Guy Carleton, commander-in-chief of British forces in North America at New York, relates to: an inquisition into the murder of Captain Huddy; the treatment of German prisoners; and the granting of a passport for a vessel to proceed from Philadelphia with provisions for American naval prisoners. The American Revolutionary War was essentially not one war but two.

First, there was a civil war with the American Colonies, beginning in 1775 and ending at Yorktown (Virginia) in October 1781; and then there was a second war, which started in 1778 when France (and later Spain and the Dutch Republic) entered the conflict in support of the Patriot cause. This conflict would last until September 1783, when the Treaty of Paris was ratified. During the second war, Joshua 'Jack' Huddy, the commander of a New Jersey Patriot militia unit, was summarily hanged in April 1782 by pro-British Associated Loyalist irregulars – an event that became a motive force behind one of the first international incidents of the fledgling USA.

As an officer, Huddy had been removed from British custody at New York by a band of regional Loyalists, ostensibly for the purpose of making a prisoner exchange. However, no such exchange was forthcoming. More than 400 people eventually gathered to protest at his execution, and a petition was sent to General Washington demanding retribution. Both Washington and Carleton condemned the hanging and prompted the British to forbid the removal of any further prisoners.

George Washington.

As early as February 1776, Reading (Pennsylvania) was already receiving German prisoners in the service of the British Crown. Prior to 1781 the majority of these Hessian or Brunswick mercenaries were officers, and although prisoners of war (POWs) were not allowed to leave their barracks without permission, grants of parole allowed many officers to go to Philadelphia or New York. However, many private soldiers escaped and made their way back to the British lines, as the mostly German-American citizens of Reading were harsher in their treatment of their own countrymen than they were of English, Scottish or Canadian prisoners.

American prisoners were not legally recognised by Parliament as 'prisoners of war' until March 1782 (six months after the British surrender at Yorktown by Cornwallis), a status that allowed them to be detained, released or exchanged. This method of dealing with 'rebel' prisoners provided Britain with a free hand to deal with her captives by any method she saw fit. Moreover, the appalling conditions aboard British prison ships (such as the *Whitby* and the *Jersey*) were well known to the Continental Congress at Philadelphia, and had led many American sailors to enlist in the Royal Navy out of desperation.

Although the British commissary of naval prisoners suggested that American marine prisoners coud be exchanged for British soldiers, Washington refused to negotiate as it would have provided the British with considerable reinforcements (of troops) and would have caused a depletion of prisoners in American hands available for exchange. What's more, this would also have provided no benefits to the Continental war effort as most of the American naval captives in New York were from privateering vessels.

Head Quarters 24th Decr 1782

Sir

      I have been favored with your Excellency's three several Letters of the 11th & 12th instant: covering the report of the Judge Advocate of your Army, respecting a farther inquisition which had been proposed to be made into the Murder of Capt. Huddy; a representation of Lieut. Reinking relative to the treatment of the German Prisoners at Reading, and a Passport for a Vessell to proceed from Philadelphia to New York, with necessaries for our Naval Prisoners.

      I should have done myself the honor of acknowledging the receipt of these Despatches some days sooner, had I been my self sufficiently possessed of the facts,

to

His Excellency Sir Guy Carleton.

to have given so particular & explicit
an Answer to Mr. Reinking's representation
as I wished, without having recourse
to the Gentleman who is immediately
concerned in the safe keeping the Prisoners
of War — having obtained a reply from
the Secretary at War to my letter on this
subject, I now take the liberty of inclosing
a copy of it to your Excellency —

I am much obliged by your mentioning the state of the American Marine
Prisoners — As the management of that
business was properly in the Department
of the Agent of Marine, I have given
an extract of your Letter to Mr. Morris,
and flatter myself the necessary relief
will be provided for them without delay

6538 (3)

Some time previous to the receipt
of your Letter, in which you mention the
situation of Captain Schaack, permission
had been given for that Gentleman to go
into New York on Parole, and I am unacquainted with the reasons which have
prevented his arrival at that place—

I have the honor to be
Sir Your Excellency's

Most Obedient and
very humble Servant
G Washington

Head Quarters 24th Decr 1782

Sir

I have been favored with your Excellency's three several letters of the 11th and 12th instant covering the report of the Judge Advocate of your Army, respecting a further inquisition which had been proposed to be made into the murder of Capt. Huddy; a representation of Lieut. Reinking relative to the treatment of the German prisoners at Reading, and a Passport for a vessel to proceed from Philadelphia to New York, with necessaries for our Naval Prisoners.

I should have done myself the honor of acknowledging the receipt of these Despatches some days sooner, had I been myself sufficiently possessed of the facts, to have given so particular or explicit an answer to Mr. Reinking's Representation as I wished, without having recourse to the Gentleman who is immediately concerned in the safekeeping the Prisoners of War — having obtained a reply from the Secretary at War to my letter on this subject, I now take the liberty of inclosing a Copy of it to your Excellency —

I am much obliged by your mentioning the state of the American Marine Prisoners As the management of that business was properly in the department of the Agent of Marine, I have given an extract of your Letter to Mr Morris, and flatter myself the necessary relief will be provided for them without delay.

Some time previous to the receipt of your Letter, in which you mention the situation of Captain Schaack, permission had been given for that Gentleman to go into New York on Parole, and I am unacquainted with the reasons which have prevented his arrival at that place.

      I have the honor to be
        Sir
           Your Excellency
              Most obedient and
                very humble Servant
                  George Washington

A complex command
Horatio Nelson to William Marsden, Secretary of the Admiralty

7 AUGUST 1804

In May 1803, ahead of renewed hostilities between Britain and France, Horatio Nelson
was appointed commander-in-chief of the Mediterranean. Aged forty-four, he was the
youngest ever given this command in Royal Navy history. A proven exceptional battle-
fleet commander, having had successes at the battles of the Nile (1798) and
Copenhagen (1801), this appointment was to be his sternest test in twenty-three
years of naval service.

Nelson was tasked to blockade Napoleon's French Mediterranean fleet at Toulon
and, if it escaped, to destroy it, thus safeguarding Britain from Napoleon's invasion
threat. Additionally he had to: defend the Strait of Gibraltar; protect British seaborne
trade; maintain diplomatic relationships; gather intelligence; cultivate relations with
potential European allies; and keep in check French and Dutch enemies while also
monitoring potential future enemies such as Spain.

Balancing the competing demands of this complex command, Nelson also had
to ensure the provisioning and fighting efficiency of his ships and the health of men
serving in this fleet. He was to achieve this initially with only nine ships, in a vast
theatre extending '3,000 miles from Cape St Vincent, Portugal to the Levant' without
modern communication systems and virtually independent from British government
control – Toulon being more than 2,000 miles from London, and 600 and 700 miles
respectively from the only British naval Mediterranean bases, Gibraltar and Malta.
Nelson met these expectations by serving on his flagship, HMS *Victory*, at sea for
nearly two years without setting foot on land, and by bringing to the fore his
administrative skills and attention to detail.

This is evidenced in a letter dated 7 August 1804 by Nelson to William Marsden,
Secretary of the Admiralty. Typically direct, it reveals different facets of Nelson's
workload and character, highlighting his authority in handling significant operational
issues. The importance of the contract agreed by Doctor Snipe and Surgeon Gray for
30,000 gallons of lemon juice – an effective preventative against scurvy, and beneficial
for his men's health – shows Nelson's practical knowledge of its cost in England and its
inferior quality to that produced in Messina, Sicily, but also that buying it from Messina
would result in savings to the public purse as it was closer to where his ships were

Horatio Nelson.

stationed. It also reveals Nelson's trust in Snipe and Gray to negotiate such a contract; allowing colleagues to act on their initiative strengthened bonds with peers and was a classic Nelson leadership trait.

Nelson's sense of honour and devotion to public duty entailed a constant keeping of his finger on the pulse. This is highlighted by his comments concerning the 'impropriety' of two pursers dismissed from their previous employment due to 'improper conduct' to positions of relative importance in 'public situations abroad'.

Nelson's expressed views about prisoners of war, considering his perceived ruthlessness in battle, are revelatory. His hatred of the French inculcated by his mother when he was a boy is well known: indeed, in 1793 Nelson famously told a midshipman on HMS *Agamemnon* 'you must hate a Frenchman as much as you hate the devil.' Perhaps this sentiment is not surprising given that for much of his lifetime France had been at war with Britain and that Napoleon represented everything diametrically opposite to his political and monarchical beliefs.

Despite this, however, this letter reveals Nelson's humane side – often lauded by his fellow officers and men – which was extended to enemies, including the hated French. For instance, he informed the governor of Barcelona on 16 November 1804: 'it is the duty of individuals to soften the horrors of war as much as possible' and this humanitarianism underpins his assertions:

'as prisoners of war are not allowed wine, the giving them salt beef instead of fresh, will from their long and close confinement naturally produce disease and many dangerous consequences, and it is with much deference I take the liberty of mentioning to their Lordships (that as French men are in the habit of drinking small wine in their own country) the propriety of allowing prisoners of war a certain quantity each per day'.

The overriding testimony to Nelson's efficacy as commander-in-chief of the Mediterranean was the stunning victory by his fleet at the Battle of Trafalgar on 21 October 1805, which thwarted Napoleon's invasion plans of Britain and established Britain's undisputed mastery at sea for more than a century.

Victory at Sea 7th August 1804–

(R. 4 Octr)

Sir

I herewith transmit You Copies of a
Contract entered into by Doctor Snipe Physician
of the Fleet and Mr. Gray Surgeon of the Naval
Hospital at Malta, with Mr. John Broadbent
Merchant at Messina, for supplying Thirty
thousand Gallons of Lemon juice for the
Sick and Hurt Board, which You will
please to lay before the Lords Commissioners
of the Admiralty for their information, as
it appears to me from the low price
Contracted for, to be an object of great con=
sideration in the Victualling department,
and by which immense Sums might be

saved

William Marsden Esqr.

saved by that Board in their future purchase of this Article, which I understand from the Physician of the Fleet may be had in any Quantity.

I must here beg to observe that Doctor Snipe went from Malta (where he was on Service) to Messina for the purpose of accomplishing this Contract, and when it is considered that Lemon juice in England (if so it may be called) cost eight shillings Per Gallon, and in the contract before mentioned only one shilling for the real juice, it will I am sure entitle Doctor Snipe to their Lordships approbation for his conduct and perseverance on the occasion, and I understand from him that Mr. Broadbents' profits are still very fair.

I judge it proper to remark that two Pursers who have been dismissed

their

their situations for improper conduct, are both
employed at Malta, one, Mr. Woodhead
as Agent to the Hospital, and the other
Mr. Goodchild as Agent to the Contractor for
Prisoners of War, the Conduct of the former
has already been extremely improper as
represented by Doctor Snipe to the Sick
and Hurt Board, and it will naturally
occur to their Lordships the impropriety of
appointing such Characters to public situ-
:ations abroad.

I am informed it is the
intention of the Agent to the Contractor for
Prisoners of War to discontinue giving
them fresh Beef, and to supply them
with Salt in lieu, on account of the latter
being so much more reasonable than the
former. I must therefore beg to observe

to

to their Lordships, that as prisoners of War
are not allowed Wine, the giving them salt
Beef instead of fresh, will from their long
and close confinement naturally produce
disease and many dangerous consequences;
and it is with much deference I take the
liberty of mentioning to their Lordships (that
as FrenchMen are in the habit of drinking
small wine in their own Country) the
propriety of allowing Prisoners of War a
certain quantity each per day.

I am
Sir
Your most Obedient
humble Servant

Nelson & Bronte

Victory at Sea 7th August 1804

Sir,

      I herewith transmit you Copy of a contract entered into by Doctor Snipe Physician of the Fleet and Mr Gray Surgeon of the Naval Hospital at Malta, with Mr John Broadbent Merchant at Messina, for supplying Thirty thousand Gallons of Lemon juice for the Sick and Hurt Board, which you will please to lay before the Lords Commissioners of the Admiralty for their information, as it appears to me from the low price contracted for, to be an object of great consideration in the Victualling department, and by which immense Sums might be saved by that Board in their future purchase of this Article, which I understand from the Physician of the Fleet may be had in any Quantity.

      I must here beg to observe that Doctor Snipe went from Malta (where he was on Service) to Messina for the purpose of accomplishing this Contrait [contract], and when it is considered that Lemon juice in England (if so it may be called) cost eight shillings per Gallon, and in the contract before mentioned only one Shilling for the real juice, it will I am sure entitle Doctor Snipe to their Lordships approbation for his conduct and perseverance on the occasion, and I understand from him that Mr Broadbent's profits are still very fair.

I judge it proper to remark that two Pursers who have been dismissed their situations for improper conduct, are both employed at Malta, one, Mr Woodhead as Agent to the Hospital, and the other Mr Goodchild as Agent to the Contractor for Prisoners of War, the conduct of the former has already been extremely improper as represented by Doctor Snipe to the Sick and Hurt Board, and it will naturally occur to their Lordships the impropriety of appointing such Characters to Public Situations abroad.

I am informed it is the intention of the Agent to the Contractor for Prisoners of War to discontinue giving them fresh Beef, and to supply them with Salt in lieu, an account of the latter being so much more reasonable than the former, I must therefore beg to observe to Their Lordships, that as Prisoners of War are not allowed Wine, the giving them Salt Beef instead of fresh, will from their long and close confinement naturally produce disease and many dangerous consequences, and it is with much deference I take the liberty of mentioning to their Lordships (that as French Men are in the habit of drinking small wine in their own Country) the propriety of allowing Prisoners of War a certain quantity each per day.

I am

Sir

Your Most Obedient

humble Servant

Nelson & Bronte

'The Lane down to your farm is dark...'
Words of warning during the Swing Riots

1830

Revolution is often seen as something that starts in cities and in the nineteenth century Britain's rulers warily watched the urban working classes, fearing that these men and women crammed higgledy-piggledy into filthy towns would explode like a tinder box, demanding greater rights.

However, in the winter of 1830–1831, the greatest threat to the ruling classes in fact came from desperate, disenfranchised agricultural workers in rural southern England, who unleashed a wave of fire and fury popularly known as the Swing Riots.

Swing was a product of economic distress. The end of the Napoleonic Wars in 1815 had led to a contraction in Britain's internal and European markets, as well as an influx of workers demobilised from the armed forces.

The fifteen years that followed were ones of low wages, bad harvests, discontent and disorder. Groups and demonstrations calling for parliamentary reform flourished and were often violently supressed, as was the case at the 1819 Peterloo Massacre in Manchester. This period also saw genuine rising and attempts at violent revolution, such as the abortive Pentrich Rising in 1817.

In 1830, agricultural labourers in the south of England were in dire straits. Failed harvests and the introduction of labour-saving threshing machines led to less work, lower wages and higher prices. Many were left without the means of subsistence.

In November 1830 in Kent, where this letter to Thomas Hodges MP was sent, these downtrodden men began what became a spontaneous wave of disorder and insurrection that spread across southern England and into the Midlands.

Under the banner of the mythical Captain Swing, the rioters destroyed threshing machines, burned down barns and other buildings, and threatened violence on landowners, whether by a mob surrounding a house or the sending of a threatening letter such as this one.

One commentator observed that it seemed the men sought 'to strike back terror upon the terrorists' but the rioters had clear demands, too: better wages, the destruction of the threshing machinery that took their work, and a reduction of tithes paid to the church, which depleted their already meagre wages.

A mob in Kent burning a hayrick during the Swing Riots.

Letters like this were typical of the tactics, but they were empty threats. Despite the promise that 'I kills you' and claims that special constables would be shot, few Swing rioters were armed at all and the only person to die during the disturbances was himself a rioter.

This letter is interesting in that the writer claims to be French but is probably not: the poor spelling and grammar is almost certainly due to illiteracy. It is likely that the writer is merely pretending to be French in an attempt to strike further terror into the letter's recipient – France had had its own revolution in July 1830 and there were fears that French agents were directing the riots.

The Swing Riots were not successful. Promises made to pay higher wages while they were happening were quickly rescinded afterwards. Nineteen rioters were hanged, more than 600 imprisoned and almost 500 transported to Australia. However, the Riots did hasten the collapse of the Duke of Wellington's government, allowing Earl Grey's Whig administration to introduce the 1832 Great Reform Act, beginning the long road to universal suffrage in Britain.

Mawry Street Hotel de France,

J. French

My spelling is bad but de French are not so English.

I write you these few lines nearly to give you warning, I'm one of 3 thousand who mean to pull down to de ground your house which is called Bempstead next week. And dip your head in debtors fret ways you think dat soldiers will freem us no no I tell you. Monsieur with his sussex friends will rout 10 Thousand red herrins, you may tarke into Your heart dat we will come. Monsieur will not dreme de English lie upon it, if we do not come, de moon does not shine nor de stars look bright to night. my men will soon shoot 56 of your special connables. — — — —

— The Lane down to your farm is dark — we will light it up. All your tenants farms are Dark

Sulphur & Wheat dilds
Staplehurst W. rotham Iden Northeant Southeant

                    Charity Street Hotel de France

My spelling is bad but de [sic] French are not

    so English.

        I write you these few lines meerley to give

you warning. I'm one of 3 thousand who mean to pull to de

ground your house which is called Hemstedd next week and dip

your head in de horse fuel. Maye you think that soldiers will

find us, no no I kills you. Monsieur with his sussix friend will

rout 10 thousand red herrings. You may harke into your hearts

dasire with Colne Monsieur will not deceive de English be upon

it, if we do not come de moon does not shire nor de stars look

bright to night. My man will soon shoot 50 of your special

constables-----------

        The Lane down to your farm is dark-

            we will light it up.

        All your tenants farms are Dark.

            Ditto

    Sulphuring W[ith] heat — J S   Now only one

[one line illegible]

The little things count
The War Office to Lord Kitchener on provision for Indian troops

14 DECEMBER 1915

Approximately 1.3 million Indian soldiers served in the First World War, and more than 74,000 of these lost their lives. In the first few months of the war in particular, the Indian Army played a vital role: at a time when Britain was still recruiting and training volunteers, soldiers from across the Empire came to fight on the Western Front and support the British cause. The Indian Army provided the largest number of troops, and by the end of 1914 they made up almost one-third of the British Expeditionary Force.

Indian troops first arrived in France from the end of September 1914. Here they were greeted with flowers and gifts, a signal that the French were very grateful for their contribution.

A further sense of gratitude was extended when the Indian Comforts Fund was set an express target to provide comforts to Indians serving on the Western Front who were unable to go home. In correspondence from Sir Walter Lawrence (who had been appointed Commissioner for the Welfare of Indian Troops) to Lord Kitchener (Secretary of State for War), we are given an insight into how this affected the spirits of these Indian soldiers.

Lawrence writes to Kitchener on 14 December 1915 saying that the little things count and that the Indians are impressed by the care taken about their religious observances – which include a temporary mosque and arrangements for reading holy scriptures.

Similar arrangements were being made back in England, with the Royal Pavilion in Brighton being converted into a hospital for wounded soldiers. From 1914 to 1916, this was used for Indian soldiers who had been wounded on the Western Front; the architectural style of the building and interior was deemed appropriate for making Indian soldiers feel at home while they were convalescing. The first patients arrived early in December 1914, and over the next year around 2,300 Indian patients were treated there.

It wasn't just the medical needs of the patients that were catered for though: again, a lot of effort was taken to cater for religious and cultural needs. Muslims and Hindus were provided with separate water supplies; nine kitchens were set up to cater for the different religious and caste traditions relating to food; and different areas for prayer were established around the site. Arrangements were also made for those who died in the hospital – with a site for open-air cremations for Sikhs and Hindus at Patcham, and a special cemetery in Woking for Muslims.

The letter suggests that all of this had a positive effect on the morale of the troops of the Indian Army, and that the men themselves were very pleased with how they were being treated.

108th Indian Field Ambulance,
Gallipoli, 1915.

94 Eaton Square, S.W.,

14th December 1915.

My dear Lord Kitchener.

Since my last letter to you dated the 2nd October I have paid two visits to France and have been in constant touch with the Indian Hospitals in England. When it was decided to move the Indian Infantry Divisions from France, steps were at once taken to evacuate as soon as possible Indian Hospitals in England and in France. The first Hospital to be closed was the Mont Dore Hospital at Bournemouth. The patients and the personnel were both moved to Brighton. The Kitchener Hospital was next evacuated, and the intention is to keep the Pavilion at Brighton and the Lady Hardinge Hospital at Brockenhurst, the latter of which will be the last Indian Hospital in England to close. In France the Hospitals at Boulogne and Hardelot have been closed, and the patients have been moved into

the

the Hospital at Montreuil, which will be maintained for
the purposes of the Indian Cavalry.   To it will be attached a Convalescent Depot and the Reinforcing section.   The
Convalescent Depot at Boulogne has been moved into the
Reinforcing base, and both will gradually disappear.
There is a small Hospital at Rouen, which consists of tents
and provides for a number of details stationed at Rouen -
some 864 men.   It has 107 beds.   This Hospital, it is
hoped, can be reduced in size, if not dispensed with altogether.   At Marseilles one Hospital has been closed,
and it is proposed to maintain one Indian Hospital with
a Convalescent Depot.

The accommodation provided at Montreuil and at
Marseilles ought to prove ample for the requirements of
the Indian Cavalry.   I visited the area occupied by the
Indian Cavalry and was told that the normal casualties
will average between 30 and 40 per diem.   Of course if
there should be a severe action it might be well to keep
the Lady Hardinge Hospital in England as a reserve, and
officers with whom I discussed the question in France,

and

and who have had a year's experience of the working of the
Indian Hospitals, are of opinion that it would be wise, at
any rate for the present, to keep the Lady Hardinge Hospital open to Indians.

Since I last wrote to you the Hospitals in England and in France have maintained their high standard of
efficiency.   The conduct of the Sepoys has been admirable
on the whole, though I have come across cases, especially
among the Sikhs and Pathans, of men who have lost all sol-
dierly spirit.   I have noticed during the last two months
a distinct falling-off in vitality.   Men come into Hospital tired out.   There has been a noticeable increase in
phthisis.   This is attributed to exposure, and some Medical Officers suggest that it is due to crowding in billets.
The Gurkhas seem especially liable to phthisis.   One regrettable case occurred at the York Place Hospital, where
a Gurkha committed suicide.   I found two other Gurkhas
in the same Hospital very depressed.   The man who committed suicide was a Rai Limbi from the neighbourhood of Dar-
jeeling.   They are a very peculiar class and quite unlike

the

3

the other Gurkhas.   A Gurkha Native Officer rather suggested to me that the man who committed suicide was depressed
by reason of the loss of his officers and his friends. All
castes regard this long absence from India as painful
exile.   Amongst all there has been a longing to get back
to India, and I have reason to believe that some of the
desertions were not due to disloyalty or a desire to join
the enemy, but were regarded as a short cut to India and
home.   Many of them have had bad news from India: plague,
famine, threatened law-suits, anxiety about the marriage
of their daughters, and unpleasant news regarding their
wives, and general anxiety have made the Indians very rest-
less, and from enquiries which I have recently made in
Marseilles, there can be no doubt that they are all greatly elated at the idea that they are going East.   They do
not know where they are going, but I think it would be a
very wise thing before they leave Egypt if their destination were clearly explained to them.   It might be a very
dangerous thing if their destination were only disclosed
to them when they reach Aden.

              The Indians have acquired a great liking for

the French people.   The French have made much of them and
treat them more as equals than we do.   I think that the
Indians are greatly impressed with the thoroughness of the
arrangements made by our Government, and I am quite sure
that they are genuinely grateful for the treatment that
has been accorded to them in the Hospitals, both in France
and in England.   In Marseilles and in England it has been
necessary to keep the Indians under very close control.
In Marseilles the Indians compare the strict discipline
with which they are treated with the greater liberality
which is accorded to the coloured troops of France.   In
England the Sepoys have recognised that restrictions were
necessary and have accepted the regulations very well.
But the Indian personnel of the Hospitals, men for instance of the Store-keeper class, have bitterly resented
the measures taken to prevent scandals in Brighton and
elsewhere.   I have just heard on my return from France
of the attempted murder of Colonel Sir Bruce Seton.   A
Native Sub-Assistant-Surgeon walked into his office and
fired a revolver at him.   This man, I understand, was

one

5

one of the personnel which had come over from Bournemouth.
The man committed this outrage by way of protesting against
the strict discipline which has been enforced by Colonel
Sir Bruce Seton.

Both in France and in England a great deal of
work has been done to improve the various Hospitals, and
the Officers of the I.M.S. have shown great energy in improving their surroundings.   They have found useful work
for convalescent Sepoys.   This work will not be lost, for
all the Hospitals and Convalescent Depots will now be used
for British troops.   The work at Marseilles is especially
noteworthy.   Colonel Hickson, R.A.M.C., assisted by
Major Needham, I.M.S., has introduced a system of water-
supply and conservancy which is the best that I have ever
seen.   It is so good that the Maire of Marseilles and the
General Commanding the French troops have both adopted
their system for French purposes.   Major Needham is well
known as an expert on Sanitary matters.   It has been suggested that the splendid Camp at Chateau Mussot, near
Marseilles, which will be available when the Indian Infantry have left France, might be used for British Hospitals

and

and a British Convalescent Depot.   It would be a great
pity if the excellent work which has been put into that
Camp during the last year were not made use of for some
British purpose.

      In many places the French authorities have
been most sympathetic and helpful.   I would especially
mention the name of M. Cortyl of St. Venant.   He is the
Superintendent of the Lunatic Asylum there, and all officers, from Surgeon-General Macpherson, R.A.M.C., down-
wards, who have had experience of St. Venant, say that we
owe a great deal to M. Cortyl.

      Great care has been taken in France regarding
the burial and cremation of Indian Sepoys.   Colonel
Wall, I.M.S., who commanded the Boulogne Hospital, has
made an excellent cemetery in the vicinity of this Hospital.   Each grave is marked by a head-stone with the
name and regiment of the Sepoy.   In the Cemetery there
is an admirable Crematorium.   In other places the Sepoys
have been buried in special plots in various Cemeteries.
Careful records have been kept, and I hope that on historical

7.

historical and political grounds the authorities will put
up permanent head-stones when the time comes. I saw the
Adjutant-General at Headquarters recently on the subject,
and he is of opinion that it would be best to defer this
until the end of the War. I recently visited the great
Cemetery of St. Pierre at Marseilles. I found the graves
of some British soldiers, but could find no Indians. I
found that 83 Indians had been cremated at St. Pierre, and
numbers have been assigned to them on marble plaques in
the Columbarium which adjoins the Crematorium. It would
be a good thing if, instead of numbers, the names of these
men could be given. Some 46 Indians have been buried in
various Cemeteries, at St. Louise, at Le Canet, and at
Mazargues. Some have been buried in the common ground
at St. Pierre, but no names have been put up. The records
however, have been carefully kept, and there should be no
difficulty, if the authorities wish, in putting up permanent head-stones. I know from frequent conversations
with Indians of every degree that great importance is
attached by India to the graves of Indians in a foreign

country

8.

country, and I think it would be wise policy to take some trouble about this, and that it would not be a waste of money if an oriental gate were built at the Boulogne Cemetery for Indians.   It is the little things that count, and one thing which has impressed the Indians very much has been the care which has been taken about their religion and their caste observances.   They are extremely grateful for the temporary mosques and for the arrangements made for the reading of the Granth or Sikh Bible.

Yours very truly

Walter Lawrence

Field Marshal

    The Right Hon.

        Earl Kitchener of Khartoum,

            K.G., G.C.S.I., G.C.I.E., &c.

9.

Indian Field Ambulance hospital tents at Gallipoli.

Striking a blow against would-be strikers
Letter authorising the arrest of striking workers

19 FEBRUARY 1916

'In the event of a strike taking place, the Police should at once deal with the pickets by warning, by removal, and by arrest if necessary.'

In war, the domestic policies of a government at home can be just as decisive as the tactical manoeuvres of an army on the battlefield. States have always reorganised themselves to achieve their war aims: for example, income tax was first introduced in 1799 to pay for war against France.

However, in the total wars of the twentieth century, the home front became a battlefield in its own right as the British state sought to direct all of Britain's capacities towards its objectives.

To this end, conscription was introduced to fill the ranks of the armed forces, and in 1916 the Ministry of Munitions came into existence, charged with controlling the production of 'munitions of war' (not just guns and ammunition, but things like boots as well). The Ministry had oversight of thousands of factories, both publically and privately owned, and the countless workers producing munitions.

In 1914 the government had passed the Defence of the Realm Act, or DORA as it became known. This provided the government with the powers to rapidly bring regulations and penalties governing all parts of British life into law.

The regulations passed under DORA were diverse and multifarious – one even banned selling 'fresh bread', to ensure stale loaves were not wasted – but many of DORA's central provisions made serious criminals out of those who were seen as being at odds with the realm, and provided for their imprisonment and trial by court-martial.

DORA's Regulation number 42, which William Beveridge (future father of the welfare state) believed would allow policemen to arrest striking munitions workers, was one of DORA's graver edicts, allowing for the arrest and trial of those attempting to:

'Cause mutiny, sedition or disaffection ... among the civilian population, or to impede or restrict the production, repair or transport of war material or any other work necessary for the prosecution of the war.'

William Beveridge.

This regulation, initially designed with saboteurs and traitors in mind, was nearly utilised a very different way: the Ministry of Munitions, as shown in this letter, sought to use it to paint as traitors patriotic trade unionists who engaged in a strike over wages and perceived union victimisation.

Relations between munitions workers, their employers and the government were occasionally tumultuous in the First World War. Most workers and trade unions supported the war effort and made agreements to help it, but disputes still occurred and sometimes led to strikes.

In February 1916, Tom Rees, secretary of the London district of the Amalgamated Society of Engineers, fell foul of the somewhat uneasy wartime truce between the government and organised labour. Rees had agitated among workers at an Abbey Wood ammunition factory to strike over pay, and was subsequently arrested under Regulation 42 and set to stand trial at Bow Street Police court on 19 February.

Rees' case became a cause célèbre among London trade unionists (200 attended his hearing) and the government feared industrial action would be taken in sympathy, particularly at Woolwich Arsenal, so they sought advice from their lawyers on whether a man on a picket line outside his place of work could be said to 'impede the production of war material'. This was different from Rees's crime, for he was accused of not following the proper process before calling a strike, as opposed to workers deciding for themselves. The law officers were sanguine about the government's case, and so police were prepared to break the pickets.

In the end, though, this was not necessary. Rees's hearing was moved to 21 February and no strike took place at Woolwich. Charges against Rees were eventually dropped, but his case shows just how close the pressures of war brought the government to curtailing that most basic of rights – of workers to withdraw their labour.

MINISTRY OF MUNITIONS OF WAR

6 WHITEHALL GARDENS,

S.W.

February 19th, 1916.

Dear Troup,

Your letter of yesterday to Llewellyn Smith
has come to me as he is not in London. I have, however,
spoken to him on the telephone and he agrees, as regards
the question of policy raised in your letter, that it is
our desire that in the event of a strike taking place,
the Police should at once deal with the pickets by warning, by removal, and by arrest if necessary, treating
picketing as illegal under the Defence of the Realm
Regulations in this case. This was in effect the
decision of the conference last night.

As regards the point of law, I understand
that it has proved impossible to get at either of the
Law Officers, for a written opinion, to-day, but that
the Treasury Solicitor will communicate with you the
moment he can get in touch with them. What the Attorney

General

General said at our conference last night, however, was
that he thought we should have a good defence against any
action if we did treat picketing as illegal. Dennis
can no doubt tell you this as he was himself present at
the meeting.

                              Yours sincerely,

                              W H Beveridge

Siegfried Sassoon's state of mind
Letter to the editor from Brigadier-General George Cockerill

20 JULY 1918

This letter was sent to the editor of *The Nation,* a leading British radical weekly newspaper, one week after it had published a poem by the well-known poet Siegfried Sassoon.

The poem in question is entitled 'I Stood With The Dead' and is a definite statement against the war: the last verse describes the poet standing among the corpses at the Front, lamenting that these men were being paid to stand in line and to kill and to die.

In response, the letter was sent to the editor by Brigadier-General George Cockerill in order to ascertain whether or not Sassoon was fit to be back at the Front. If he had written the poem in 1918, when it was published, the author reasoned, then there were grounds to believe that Sassoon should not have been sent back to France after his stay at Craiglockhart War Hospital.

To get to this point in the story, it is worth briefly looking at Sassoon's service in the war. On 4 August 1914 he attested with the Sussex Yeomanry and by May 1915 he had been commissioned into the 3rd Battalion Royal Welch Fusiliers as second lieutenant. In the November of the same year he was posted to the 1st Battalion and sent to France. Once there, he became known for reckless acts of bravery, which eventually led to him being awarded the Military Cross in July 1916.

Throughout his military career, Sassoon had a few hospital stays, but it was the one in July 1917 that became the most significant, since the cause for this admission was stated as mental breakdown. Coinciding with this was Sassoon's statement against the war – also pictured – in which he argued that he could no longer be party to the political mistakes and insincerities for which the men were fighting and suffering. He also wanted to highlight the atrocities to all at home, who he thought could not imagine the horrors of the Front. Instead of being court-martialled for this, Sassoon was sent to Craiglockhart War Hospital in Edinburgh to undergo convalescence – because surely such an outcry against the war could only come from someone whose mind had been influenced by the war and therefore he could not be held responsible for what he had said?

Concerned that his words would be seen as those of a mad man, Sassoon decided that he had to go back to the Front, whether he wanted to or not. In due course a medical board in November 1917 declared he was fit for general duties again, and by May 1918 he was back serving on the Western Front.

The fear that the poem published in *The Nation* was written during this time, when the war was still being fought, was that Sassoon's mind might still be in chaos and that he could not be trusted with men's lives, nor trusted not to spread his anti-war sentiment. This we will never know, for in his response the editor of the newspaper does not reveal how long the poem had been in his possession before he had printed it.

Siegfried Sassoon in uniform.

122091/5 (M.I.7.)

Personal & Confidential   20th. July. 1918.

Dear Sir,

      Attention has been drawn to some verses on p. 394 of your issue of the 13th. July, 1918, signed by Siegfried Sassoon. Presumably, therefore, the author is Captain S. L. Sassoon, M.C., of the 3rd. Bn. Royal Welsh Fusiliers.

      This Officer in July 1917, was reported by a medical board to be suffering from a nervous breakdown and not responsible for his actions, but at the end of November, 1917, he was found to have recovered and to be fit for General Service. He is now serving in France.

      Your Reviewer on p. 400 of the same issue recognises clearly what was the state of Mr. Sassoon's mind when he wrote "Counter-attack and other Poems", but if Capt. Sassoon were now writing verse such as that printed on p. 394, it would appear that his mind is still chaos, and that he is not fit to be trusted with mens' lives. I should therefore be grateful if you would let me know when you received his verses "I stood with the dead". It may be, of course, that they have been in your possession some months. The information, which is desired solely in the public interest, will of course be treated as confidential.

        Yours faithfully,

          (sgd) George Cockerill

            Brig- General

            D. D. M. I.

H. W. Massingham. Esq.
  The Editor,
    "The Nation".

by

Sec. Lt. Siegfried Sassoon,

3rd Batt: Royal Welsh Fusiliers,

July, 1917.

     I am making this statement as an act of wilful defiance of
military authority because I believe that the war is being deliberately
prolonged by those who have the power to end it. I am a soldier, convinced that I am acting on behalf of soldiers. I believe that the war
upon which I entered as a war of defence and liberation has now become
a war of agression and conquest. I believe that the purposes for which
I and my fellow soldiers entered upon this war should have been so
clearly stated as to have made it impossible to change them and that had
this been done the objects which actuated us would now be attainable by
negotiation.

     I have seen and endured the sufferings of the troops and I
can no longer be a party to prolong these sufferings for ends which I
believe to be evil and unjust. I am not protesting against the conduct
of the war, but against the political errors and insincerities for which
the fighting men are being sacrificed.

     On behalf of those who are suffering now, I make this protest
against the deception which is being practised upon them; also I believe
it may help to destroy the callous complacency with which the majority
of those at home regard the continuance of agonies which they do not
share and which they have not enough imagination to realise.

Should Stalingrad receive the George Cross?
A letter from three shorthand typists to Winston Churchill

24 SEPTEMBER 1942

This letter was sent to British prime minister Winston Churchill in September 1942, but was handled by the Foreign Office, which dealt with issues relating to other countries.

During the Second World War, Hitler had launched Operation *Barbarossa* in 1941 – an operation that was central to his plan to create an empire in the east. By the end of the year the severe Russian winter had stopped the advance, but a new German offensive in 1942 began in the south as Germany and the USSR fought over the control of Stalingrad. Possession of this city was of vital strategic importance to Germany because it would have given them control of oil reserves in the Caucasus area, the River Volga, and the immense psychological advantage of capturing the city named after the Soviet leader. By the close of July 1942, the Germans had successfully broken through to the outskirts of the city, and by September, when this letter was written, they were gaining more ground in harsh conditions with high casualties.

This letter is interesting because it captures the public mood in Britain in its appreciation of the bravery of the Soviet Army and the courage of the civilian population, and highlights the significance of the Battle of Stalingrad. After the example of the bravery demonstrated by the Maltese in 1940 against German and Italian forces, the island of Malta had been given the George Cross 'for acts of the greatest heroism or for most conspicuous courage in circumstance of extreme danger'. Many people felt that the citizens of Stalingrad should also receive the same honour.

This polite, humble letter from three shorthand typists making its direct personal appeal to the prime minister was not uncommon. However, Anthony Eden, foreign secretary at the time, wrote to Winston Churchill in December 1942 and pointed out that according to the British Honours Committee, foreigners were not eligible for the award and the alternative Victoria Cross had never been given to a foreign town. Any lesser award, such as the Military Cross, 'would be difficult to explain to the Russians … in view of the precedent of Malta'.

A statue of Lenin in the centre of the ravaged city of Staliingrad *c.* 1942–43.

There was no exception made in the end to award the George Cross to the people of Stalingrad, though the city was honoured in a different way: in May 1944, a British delegation went to the Kremlin to present the city's officials with the King's Sword of Honour, a gift from George VI to the people of Stalingrad.

24th September, 1942.

The Typing Office,
Roads & Bridges Department,
Salop County Council,
County Buildings,
SHREWSBURY, Shropshire. 4

Dear Mr. Churchill,

We wish to refer to the heroic defence of the city of Stalingrad.

We feel sure that every man, woman and child in the British Empire would like to show some appreciation of the wonderful way in which this Russian city has been and is being defended against the huge and barbarous German armies pitted against her. We most humbly beg to suggest that as in the case of Malta, some recognition of the valour of our allies the Russian soldiers, airmen and civilians be made to that city in a similar way whatever the outcome of this gigantic struggle may be.

We are but three shorthand-typists working in a government office but we are confident that you will listen to this, our suggestion, and we do hope and trust that you will give this matter your consideration.

With every good wish for your health and happiness,
We are,
Your obedient servants,

████████████ (age 16)
████████████ (age 20)
E. Joan Donkin. (age 23)

Map showing the position of Russian forces during Operation Barbarossa.

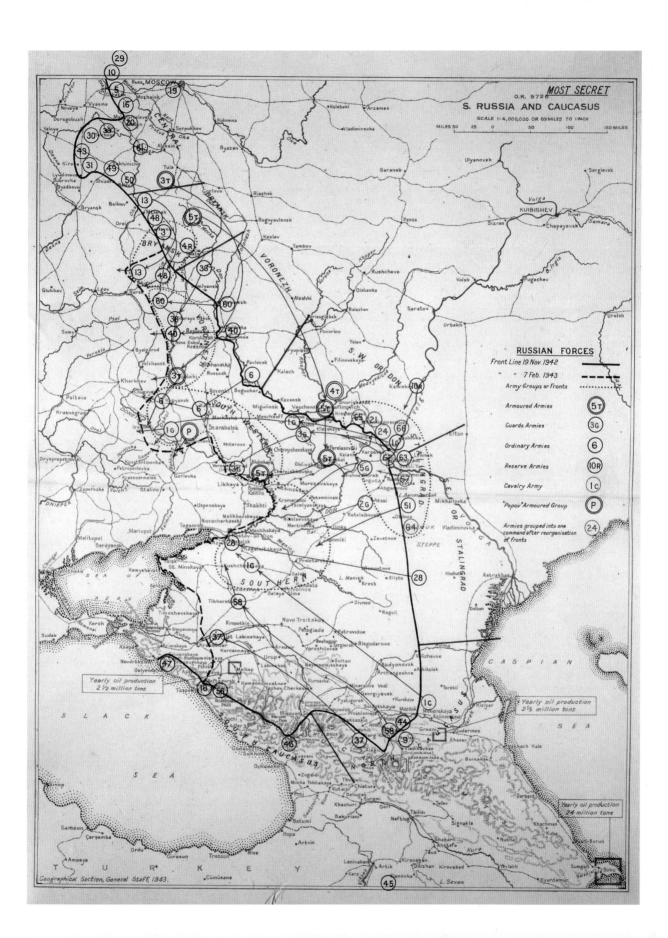

Churchill and the macaques of Gibraltar
Correspondence concerning ape welfare

1944

Situated on the southern coast of the Iberian Peninsula and guarding the entrance to the Mediterranean, the island of Gibraltar is home to the Barbary macaque, the only species of wild monkey found in Europe.

In 1713, Gibraltar was ceded to the British under the terms of the Treaty of Utrecht. Soon after Britain had assumed control of the island, a belief emerged that Gibraltar would remain under British rule for as long as the Barbary apes were still there: when the apes left the Rock, the British would soon follow. The British Army soon established a garrison and naval base on the island and assumed responsibility for managing the macaque population. However, by 1913 the number of macaques had been reduced to single figures. To reverse the decline, therefore, the governor of Gibraltar, Sir Alexander Godley, quickly brought over eight young female apes from North Africa to replenish the population.

In 1915 the Gibraltar regiment appointed a 'Keeper of the Apes' who was given responsibility for the upkeep of the colony and maintaining a register. Updated every week, this register contained individual entries for each macaque, noting their names (many in honour of brigadiers, colonels and government officials and their wives), birthdays, weight, dietary requirements and offspring. The colony was also granted an official food allowance, which in 1944 amounted to £4 a month, which was used to supplement the monkeys' natural diet with a variety of vegetables, fruit and nuts.

'Scruffy' developed dictatorial tendencies and had to be locked up to protect the local community.

Winston Churchill, who had visited Gibraltar, was keenly aware of the legend. In the early days of the Second World War, learning that the macaque population had dwindled to seven, he therefore issued instructions to have six females brought in quickly from Morocco.

A few years later, on 22 August 1944, Churchill asked for an update on the situation: 'The Prime Minister is most anxious that they should not be allowed to die out, a possibility about which he has heard disquieting rumours. I believe there are dire prophecies about what will happen to Gibraltar if the apes vanished.'

In response, the governor of Gibraltar reported that the perilous position of the Rock apes was only a rumour. The number of macaques was currently fourteen, which included the six females imported from Morocco. He had also been reliably informed that the 'marriage' between 'Pat' and 'Bessie' had been recently consummated and that hopes were high for a new arrival to the colony.

In September, the prime minister issued a directive to the colonial secretary: 'The establishment of the apes on Gibraltar should be twenty-four, and every effort should be made to reach this number as soon as possible and maintain it thereafter.' To carry out his instructions, a troop transport was dispatched to North Africa and additional apes were brought to Gibraltar.

Churchill's determination to prevent the apes from disappearing from Gibraltar was not based solely on superstition: he was aware of the symbolic importance of the apes and their effect on British morale. In the midst of war, their disappearance would have been seized upon by Hitler's propaganda machine in an attempt to demoralise the British population.

Today, the population of the colony exceeds 300 animals, which are divided into five troops. For many, the Gibraltar Barbary macaques are considered to be the top tourist attraction in Gibraltar and a potent symbol of Britain's sovereignty over the island.

Two comparative photgraphs showing the transformation of land near the Rock from a race course to an airport.

21 August, 1944.

Dear Thornley,

Would you let us have a
report about the welfare of the
apes in Gibraltar? The Prime
Minister is most anxious that
they should not be allowed to
die out, a possibility about
which he has heard disquieting
rumours. I believe there are
dire prophecies about what
would happen to Gibraltar if
the apes vanished.

Yours sincerely,

C.H. Thornley, Esq.,
Colonial Office.

*Await further
from C.O.
423*

Mr. [illegible] attached

25th August, 1944.

Dear Colville,

With reference to your letter
of the 21st August about the apes in
Gibraltar, we have no information
later than September, 1943, when the
Governor said that in November 1942
the apes started to die off in an
alarming manner. We understand that
in the winter 1942-3 their number
fell from 16 to 5, possibly from
pneumonia. The Governor
accordingly arranged for
reinforcements to be brought from
North Africa and for better
accommodation to be provided.

We have, however, asked the
Governor by telegram to let us know
the facts as they are at present.

Yours sincerely,

C. Thornley

Private Secretary.

J.R. Colville, Esq.

(4)

PRIME MINISTER'S
PERSONAL MINUTE

SERIAL No. *M.95/4.*

<u>COLONIAL SECRETARY</u>.

      The establishment of the apes should be 24,
and every effort should be made to reach this number as
soon as possible and maintain it thereafter.

W.S.C.

1.9.44

PRIME MINISTER

P.M.
2

You wished to be

reminded about

Gibraltar and the

apes.

Ask for Chi
2 15/7
a report.

They must not die out
P.O. Cope? Chi 18/8

Keeping up Blitz spirits
Letter about the state of air-raid shelters

OCTOBER 1940

From September 1940 until the following May, London was dominated by the Blitz. This was the German bombing offensive – the name of which was derived from the German term blitzkrieg (lightning war) – that targeted the capital and other large ports and industrial centres across Britain.

Earlier in the same year the government had begun to build communal public air-raid shelters. These were designed to hold large groups of people and were an alternative for those living in built-up areas without gardens in which they could erect Anderson shelters.

Public shelters were constructed from brick and concrete and were identified by large black signs marked with a white 'S', so they could be easily found in the blackout. They were divided into different areas and furnished with wooden bunks.

Jenny Fleming, who frequently sought shelter in a public air-raid shelter in Leinster Square, West London, wrote to the Home Secretary, Herbert Morrison, in 1940. In her letter she describes some of the hardships that she and others who used the shelter had to endure. Listed among her concerns are the issues of lighting, lack of reading material, the diminishing number of marshals, the leaking roof and the hard wooden benches provided for sitting and sleeping on. She writes that if the benches could be replaced with comfortable bunks, then the former could be used as exhibits in a 'museum of instruments of torture'. Earlier in the letter she describes them as a 'secret-means, purposely devised [by Hitler] to break our morale!'

Jenny's letter is eloquently written, detailing each point in turn, and frequently suggests solutions to many of the problems. For example, her concern that all of the lights except for one small electric one are automatically extinguished is accompanied by a straightforward solution: she suggests there should be a room that is dimly lit for those who want to rest and can 'sleep through bombs' even if the shelter is shaking so much 'that you expect it to collapse at any minute', and another more brightly lit area for those who cannot sleep. Jenny has drawn a small diagram of the space to illustrate her idea, and swings from a slightly comical description of the heaviest sleepers to the more desperate feelings of those who stay awake throughout the night. 'If you sit in this dim light the night through, waiting for bombs, feeling the tremors of the earth beneath your feet … such a night seems endless!'

She also writes passionately about the roof and how it needs to be made rainproof 'at once!', and describes the prison-like walls of the shelter and how they could be made 'friendlier' with posters of the British fleet of planes to 'fortify morale'. She also comments on the kindness of the marshals and how more are needed. Throughout her letter, there is stoicism and a tendency to make the best of things, along with a concern for others and a strong desire to see the government make improvements, before 'everybody' becomes 'depressed and miserable'.

What makes her letter all the more powerful are the beautiful illustrations of the different challenges she describes in the shelters. These add another dimension, bringing a vivid image of human suffering to the letter. The pictures of the woman sitting shivering under the umbrella inside the shelter, a look of misery on her face, or the woman wrapped up against the cold struggling to read in the dim light, make Jenny's words more poignant.

Having fun in an air raid shelter.

From further documents within the file, including more illustrations, we learn that following the receipt of her letter Herbert Morrison spoke to Jenny on the telephone about the shelter's conditions. He duly made arrangements to visit the shelter (although a further letter from Jenny suggests that this did not take place), and Jenny was able to raise further concerns about conditions, including the flimsy lavatory door and the dusty concrete floor that caused breathing difficulties for the shelter's inhabitants.

23,Oktober 1940

The Ministry of security,
MR. HERBERT MORRISON.

Dear Sir,

                    I belong to the small comunity whitch
meets at every nightfall at the public shelter, in Leinster Square,
W.2.On the 17th of September I was in the same shelter, which the H.E.-
bomb honoured with its visit.And in spite of the shock(one was killed
and two wounded inside,the shelter,one of 3 sisters in a room in a
house opposite--one was killed, one wounded, one unhurt)I went there
again, night after night.The reason: It was light the whole night through

one could read and forget the nearness of danger,--there was always a
shelter-marshal, which gave you the feeling after my earlier experience that in case of danger would always be a person at hand who would
arrest at once any panic;or stop little nervious disputes with friendly tact. WHEN IT RAINED THE WATER LEEKED THROUGH,BUT WE HOPED,THIS
WOULD BE STOPPED.
                    It was damp and cold.One kind Warden brought a smal
electric stove which gave us the illusion at least, of warming the
place.
         The benches are so high, narrow and agonising that I am sure,
Hittler has -through some secret means-purposely devised it,thus to
break our morale! Since yesterday there is an order, to extinguish all
the lights, except one small electric light----not enough to let one
read, but enough to let one see the depressing surrounding, and wait
for the next shell.
              The Warden gives you as reason, that people want to
sleep and would be disturbed.
                    There are(see the plan)-2 big shelter,
with each 2 big rooms and eleven brillant lights.After 11ockl.the 4
brillant lights in the room are extinguished and only the light in the
Lav. and the cupboard stay on, and in each of those rooms is only the
wretched little lamp burning.

                    I would suggest:Keep in each of these two
big shelter, one room darkened, already after ten ockl.Those people,
who have to work next day, who are tired and sleep through bombs if
the shelter is even SO shaking that you expect it to collapse any minut
-----those people can sleep in the dim light.Give weak lights in the
4 lav. and the 2 small cupboards.
Take off the strong light lamp A, because
the contact is needed for the electric stove.
Let strong light B for those, who wants to
read.

Take out D, but
leave C. with a
dark shade, which
can be pulled down
after 11 ockl. when
people stop reading
in this part.
Please, realise, the
people in this shelter are not homeless-bombed-out ones, but mostly
those, who are frightendd with enough self-control to show their ner- *NOT*
vousness.They are reading in the papers about bombing, listening to
everyones talking about bombing, of trapped-ones, of wounded!
        If you sit in this dim light the night through, waiting for
bombs, feeling the tramours of the earth beneeth your feet, if you
hear the rattle of our own shell-splinters on the roof, the snoring
of some people, ----such a night seems <u>endless</u>!
                                        I wished we had a lib-
rary with gay short stories, old magazins in those shelters(for a
few pennies charge)_ and annimate people to read!

SHELTER-MARSHALLS.

                    There were seven.Now we have about
3 or 4. They are not paid. There is no comodity for them.They have to *Comfort*
sit, or, if they can sleep on those wooden benches, theese"Procrustes-
beds"! Too high,too narrow, too small!
                            But we need a marshal!In case
of small panics. What happens if one person gets an epileptic fit?
Or a man---we have one on the brink---gets QUITE insane suddenly?
Or a drunk man comes in to joke or molest people? or there are little
nervous fights between a lady and a Not-lady of sitting too near the
fire and keeping the warmth from the others, as there was the other day.
A nice marshal stop this in a friendly but determined way. She will
tuck those in, whimch have come uncovered, or suggest that he or she m
may sit in an empty chair belonging to somebody, which only the marshal can give permission to use to someone else.
        <u>Please try to get more marshalls, 7-10, kind and sympathetik, as</u>
<u>those we have already!</u>

        <u>The roof</u> should be made rainproof <u>at once</u> ,and
thothroughly! Saturday night we had to move about and cover the beds with
our raincoats.
        <u>The walls</u>, those depressing prison-walls, should
be made gayer, friendlier.By hanging up posters as in the underground-
stations.Those big fine posters, for instance, of our fleet or our
planes"And they will be stronger every day!"This will stimulate one, and
fortify our moral.
        <u>The benches</u> are 13 inches wide. Not more.They

consist of 2 planks--quite near to the wall and to each other. Last
night again a poor lady fell down, startled by the noise of our own
big guns.(Only bruises, nothing broken.)

    IF we should get bunks--hurray, hurray!--we shall not need
the benches and they may go to a museum of instruments of torture.

    AND IF NOT:They could be easily altered.Those detached to
the walls, have to be pushed forward, so that a 4 inch-space will be
gained. In using an iron bent-clamp from the wall, and using the deco-
ratif front-plank as the third one, with bigger intervals between each,
one can easily bring them to a size of 23-25 inches, so that one can
sleep on them without the danger of falling off. I would even shorten
the legs a bit.Women on a cushion or their mattresses finds it rather
high. The same can be said of the two middle -benches, divided by a useless piece of wood. TOO narrow to sit,TOO hard to sleep.--If A sleeps
at one side, nobody can sleep at the other, because mattresses and
cushions, being larger than 13 inches,are overflowing the other side.
And people find this nearness too unhygienic and unappetising to be so
dreadfully near to a stranger.Enlarge them too, in the same way, like
the side-benches, or lift the silly diversion and let people use generos-
ly the whole width of side I. and side II.

What about dogs in a shelter in emergency-case? Between 150 people at
least, who came in last night,--out-time-bombed from their Hotels was
a single lady with a sweet dwarf-scotty. Is she supposed to leave the
shelter and wait outside till everything is over? Or is her poor frigh
tened dog supposed to walk out by himself??The warden demanded it, he
said it was order.....funny order for a dog-worshipping people!
(The dog stayed on....his Mistress was strong and energetic looking,
like a lyoness defending her cub-----) but, would you not better give
exact orders what should happen in a case of emergency an other time?

    But whatever you do, or decide to do:
    PLEASE make it SOON!

Dont wait till everybody is gone elsewhere, or sits jittering at home.
They wont come back so quickly!We are now not more than:
DONT wait till everybody has Rhumatism or a
cold, or"Flu"!

DON_T wait till everybody is depressed
and miserable-----You DO want to help,-
dont you?

...let me appologize for my bad spelling and writing.
I am a good British subject, but unfortunately not a British-born one!

I am yours very faithfully

Jenny Fleming

(Mrs.) Jenny Fleming

15, Leinster Square, W.2.
BAYswater 0479.

TOO COLD AND WET!

TOO HIGH WITH A CUSHION!

TOO SAD WITH BARE WALLS!

TOO HARD WITHOUT A CUSHION!

TOO DARK WITH THE DIM LIGHT!

The 'Istanbul List'
The third exchange of German and Palestinian civilian internees

4 AUGUST 1944

The preliminary exchange of 46 Palestinians and 65 Germans took place on
12 December 1941. The American Embassy sent the list of Palestinians, designated
by the German government, to the High Commissioner for Palestine in Jerusalem.
The German party were escorted through Lebanon to Syria and were left by their
escorts in Aleppo as they continued to the Turkish frontier on 13 December. The
Palestinians arrived in Aleppo on 17 December, where they were provided with food
and accommodation in the French cavalry barracks, arranged by the British Security
Mission in Syria. They continued their journey and arrived in Haifa on 19 December
to be met by representatives of the Jewish Agency. Information received from the
American Embassy in Berlin indicated that the Germans were prepared to carry
out further exchanges and the Palestinian government accepted this assumption.
The Swiss took over the negotiations for future exchanges, with the Jewish Agency
supplying addresses of those eligible for exchange.

Information was communicated through the Foreign and Colonial Offices to the
German authorities through a Swiss legation in Berne; the British had no direct contact
with the German government. Decisions about the eligibility of Jews to be put on a list
of persons for exchange fell to the Jewish Agency in London. As news of the mass
deportations and murder of Jews by the Nazis spread across the world, the guidelines
were often reviewed and amended to include wives and children who were not born in
Palestine or naturalised in Palestine and whose husbands came on immigration
certificates. As this became apparent, the Jewish Agency relaxed the eligibility
guidelines even further. However, many letters were still written to the Foreign
Office pleading for relatives to be included on the list regardless of eligibility.
Many were refused.

The second exchange was scheduled to take place on 1 November 1942 but the High Commissioner for Palestine sent a telegram to the Secretary of State for the Colonies informing him that the exchange would be postponed. This was because the date was inconvenient for the Turkish authorities, the train times did not suit and it was during the Turkish holiday. As well as this, there appeared to be a shortage of accommodation in Istanbul between 1 and 11 November.

The delay troubled the British since they didn't want the Germans to think they were breaching the conditions of the exchange programme; it had been agreed that the date and place of exchange would be on 1 November in Constantinople. The exchange was confirmed on 8 October 1942 and took place on 11 November when the trains passed each other in Istanbul; 137 Palestinians arrived from Vienna to Istanbul and were exchanged for 305 Germans. Transit visas were arranged by the Turkish Ministry of Foreign Affairs.

There were two more exchanges, the last of which took place in August 1944. This took over a year to plan and recorded twenty-six Palestinians, five returning residents and 251 'refugee immigrants', of which 222 came from Bergen-Belsen. A further exchange was planned but was delayed by the suggestion that Germans include men of military age. Turkey was no longer considered as an option for travel and it was agreed to wait for a common frontier with Switzerland before another exchange could be considered. On 16 September 1944 all proposals for a fourth exchange were dissolved.

The total number of Jews on the Istanbul List numbered around 1,100. Many were untraced. The files indicate that 466 Palestinian Jews were saved as a result of this exchange programme.

P o v9+21/3 B

PALESTINE,
HIGH COMMISSIONER FOR ~~TRANSJORDAN~~,
JERUSALEM. 444

4 August, 1944.

REFERENCE NO. SF/1170/39-VI.

RECEIVED
15 AUG 1944
C. O. REGY.

9-24/3/4

383

Sir,

    I have the honour to refer to your telegram
No. 478 of the 19th of April 1944 and to subsequent
correspondence regarding the proposal to effect a third
exchange of German and Palestinian civilian internees,
and to report that after a postponement of the exchange
on security grounds (see your telegram No. 669 of the   434
31st of May) arrangements were finally concluded for the
exchange to take place at Istanbul on the 5th of July.

    2.   The agreement covered the exchange of 114
Germans including 34 men, 56 women and 24 children for
283 Palestinian citizens, including 67 men, 169 women
and 47 children, the disproportion in the number of
Germans to Palestinians redressing the adverse balance
which had operated in favour of the Germans in the
composition of the second exchange. Your telegram No. 135
of the 5th February 1943 refers to this matter. As
403   intimated in your telegrams Nos. 535 of the 29th of April
408   and No. 549 of the 3rd of May the Swiss authorities were
unable to trace many of the Palestinian and near-Palestinian
citizens whose names were recorded in the official
exchange (or Istanbul) lists. In order not to jeopardise
the chances of the exchange I accepted your proposal
that the agreed number of persons to be exchanged should
be made up with persons selected from the lists of rabbis
and veteran Zionists. In the result the exchange party
included 26 Palestinian citizens, 5 returning residents
and 251 others who must be regarded as refugee immigrants.

The Right Honourable
  Oliver F.G. Stanley, P.C., M.C., M.P.,
     His Majesty's Principal Secretary of State
                  for the Colonies.   ./.

3.   The party of German nationals accompanied by
a British police escort, medical officer and nursing
staff, entrained at Affula on the evening of the 30th of
June, and proceeded via Rayak, Damascus and Aleppo to the
frontier at Meidan Ekbes where they arrived on the 3rd
of July. The German nationals were there handed over to
an official of the Turkish Government, the escort
returning to Aleppo to await the arrival of the party of
Palestinians. The party of Palestinians left Vienna on
the 2nd of July and arrived at Istanbul on the 6th July,
thereby necessitating postponement of the actual date of
exchange by one day. The Palestinians were formally
handed over to the British escort at Meidan Ekbes on the
8th of July and were transported to the reception camp
at Athlit by the direct Tripoli-Beirut-Haifa railway route,
arriving on the 10th of July. An Egyptian national was
excluded from the party at Vienna, and one Palestinian
had to be left in Istanbul on medical grounds, so that 282
persons eventually reached Palestine.

          Members of each party were allowed to take with
them 40 kilos of baggage for adults and 30 kilos for
children under 18, personal belongings such as jewellery,
family documents and photographs, and currency up to the
value of £P.10. There were no indications that the German
authorities failed to honour their agreement as regards
any of these arrangements.

4.   The accommodation provided on the narrow guage
railway from Affula in Palestine to Rayak in Syria was not
altogether satisfactory as coaches of the requisite
standard were not available. Considerations of military
security precluded the use of the more advantageous direct
Haifa-Beirut-Tripoli route for the party leaving Palestine.
The accommodation provided from Rayak to the Turkish
frontier was of a higher standard and at Meidan Ekbes the
Germans were transferred to a fully equipped sleeping car
and restaurant train. Accommodation provided for the
incoming Palestinian party was satisfactory as the security
objection to the use of the Haifa-Beirut-Tripoli route
did not exist in the case of persons coming into Palestine.

                                                    ./.

The general transportation arrangements, and
the catering undertaken by the N.A.A.F.I., were carried
through with clock-work precision and efficiency.
The smoothness which which the exchange was effected
reflects great credit on the police and military
authorities concerned. I am causing letters of appreciation to be addressed to the proper quarters.

5.   The Palestinians were physically in very poor
condition. The experiences of members of the party in
enemy-occupied territory were varied but they had no
reports to make of mass executions, gas wagons or brutal
treatment at the hands of their guards. Their chief
complaints appeared to be:-

(i)   the poor quality and insufficiency of
        the food

(ii)   the nature of the work and the long
        hours (11 hours daily)

(iii) the poor accommodation during internment.

One group of 222 persons came from the camp at
Bergen Belsen near Hanover and the other group of 62
persons from Vittel. The two groups were transferred on
the 29th June by special train to a collection centre in
Vienna. Second and third class railway accommodation
was provided for the whole of the journey from the
camps to Istanbul, and from Vienna onwards the party
had access to a sleeping car (for the aged and sick) and
two dining cars. The food consisted of bread, oleo-
margarine, liver paste and water. Two doctors were in
attendance on the party. The only guards were a few
green-uniformed S.S. men.

6.   In view of the great interest displayed locally
in this matter and constant appeals by the relatives of
Palestinians still detained in enemy territory, I am glad

./.

to note from your telegram No.955 of the 1st
August that negotiations for the fourth exchange
of Germans and Palestinians are proceeding.

? on
9421/3ᶜ

        I have the honour to be,
            Sir,
          Your most obedient,
            humble servant,

for
       HIGH COMMISSIONER (on tour).
       FOR PALESTINE.

*Signed by the Chief Secretary for
the High Commissioner on tour.*

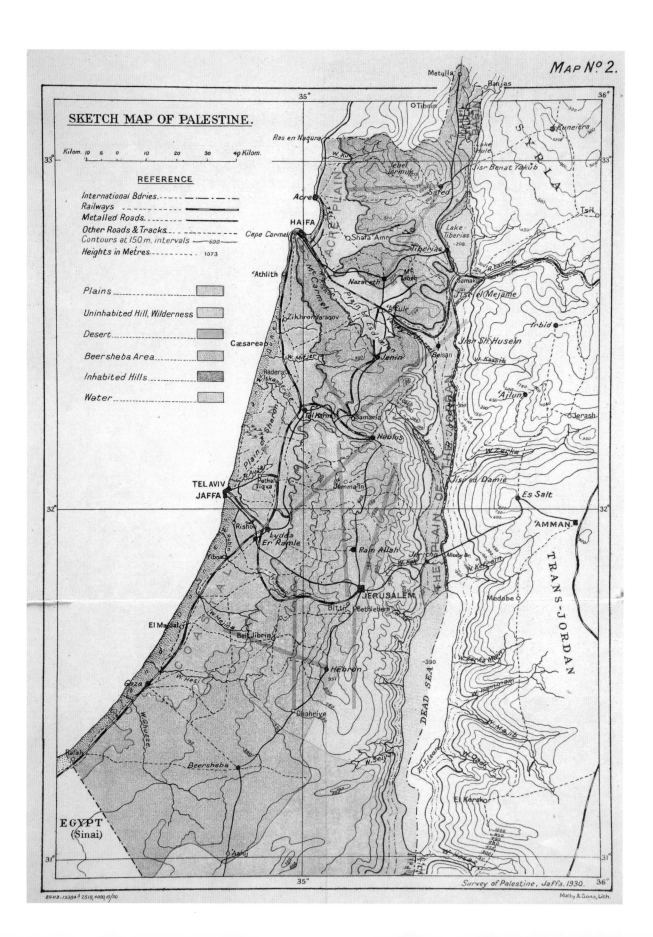

MAP No 2.

SKETCH MAP OF PALESTINE.

Kilom. 10 5 0   10   20   30   40 Kilom.

REFERENCE

International Bdries............. -------
Railways ....
Metalled Roads..............
Other Roads & Tracks............. -------
Contours at 150 m. intervals ——600——
Heights in Metres............. 1073

Plains ....
Uninhabited Hill, Wilderness ....
Desert ....
Beersheba Area ....
Inhabited Hills ....
Water ....

Metulla
Banias
O Tibnin
Ras en Naqura
W. Kurn
ACRE PLAIN
Jebel Jermuk
Safed
S Y R I A
Kuneitra
Lake Hule
Jisr Benat Yakub
Tsil
Acre
HAIFA
Cape Carmel
O Shafa 'Amr
Lake Tiberias
Tiberias
Mt Carmel
Nazareth
Mt Tabor
Plain of Esdraelon
Samakh
R. Yarmuk
Jisr el Mejame
'Athlith
Afule
Irbid
Zikhron Ya'aqov
Jenin
Jisr Sh. Husein
Beisan
W. Kassib
Cæsarea
W. Mifjer
'Ajlun
Hadera
W. Iskenderune
Jerash
Plain of Sharon
Tul Karm
Samaria
Nablus
W. Zerka
Jisr ed Damie
Pethah Tiqva
Semma'in
Es Salt
TEL AVIV
JAFFA
Rishon
AMMAN
Lydda
Er Ramle
Ram Allah
Jericho
Allenby Br.
W. Kefrein
TRANS-JORDAN
Yibna
W. Rubin
JERUSALEM
Bittir
Bethlehem
Medabe
El Majdal
Beit Jibrin
Hebron
Gaza
W. Hesi
Dhahriye
DEAD SEA
W. Zerka Main
-390
W. Hammam
W. Ghuzze
Beersheba
W. Sein
El Lisan
W. Dada
EGYPT
(Sinai)
Rafah
El Kerak
Ashi
W. Hesa

Malby & Sons, Lith.

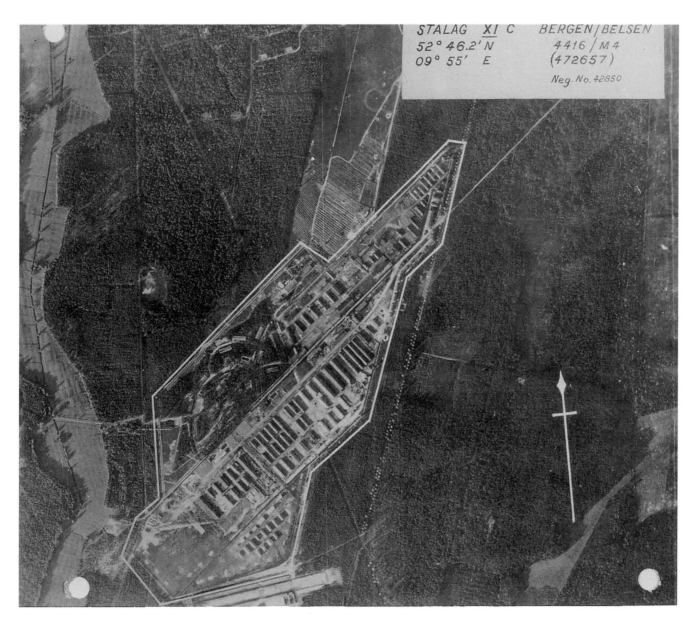

STALAG XI C BERGEN/BELSEN
52° 46.2' N   4416 / M4
09° 55' E   (472657)

Neg. No. 42850

An aerial view of the Bergen-Belsen
concentration camp, taken in 1944.

Relations and
relationships

Advice well received
Princess Elizabeth's letter to her stepmother, Katherine Parr

SUMMER 1548

Henry VIII died on 28 January 1547 and by June the same year his widow, Katherine, had taken a new husband, Lord Admiral Thomas Seymour, Baron Seymour of Sudeley. This hasty action worsened the relationship that Katherine and Thomas had with his brother, Edward Seymour, Duke of Somerset, lord protector and governor of Edward VI. Nonetheless, Katherine still managed to secure the guardianship of Elizabeth, who resided with Katherine at her dower manors of Hanworth (West London) and Chelsea (inner London). This was an interesting situation, as it had been rumoured that only a few weeks prior to his proposal to Katherine, Thomas had asked Elizabeth to marry him and she had refused. Nonetheless, the evidence suggests that Elizabeth was not ill disposed to Thomas's attentions and that there had been some level of intimacy between them while she was living within the household.

Katherine was pregnant with her daughter, Mary, by December 1547 and scandalous rumours were circulating about the nature of the relationship between Elizabeth and Thomas by the first half of 1548. This letter was probably written in early summer 1548, since Elizabeth makes reference to the fact that Katherine was unwell at the time – perhaps as a result of the later stages of her pregnancy. Prior to writing this letter, Elizabeth had been sent to Cheshunt, Hertfordshire, to live in the household of Sir Anthony Denny, a close friend of the late Henry VIII – a move that would have both removed the opportunity for the relationship to develop between Elizabeth and Thomas and protected Elizabeth's reputation.

The letter suggests that Katherine had given Elizabeth guidance about the dangers that could arise from gossip and that she was taking it on board: 'I weighed it more deeper when you said you would warn of all evils that you should hear of me.' Elizabeth clearly looked upon Katherine with respect and love and signed the letter: 'Your highness's humble daughter', which provides an interesting insight into the nature of the relationship between these two royal women.

THARINE PARRE

25

Although I coulde not be plentiful in giuinge thankes for the manifolde kindenis receyue
at your hithnis hande at my departure, yet I am some thinge to be borne with al, for
truly I was replete with sorowe to departe frome your highnis, especially leuinge you
vndoubtful of helthe, and albeit I answered litel I wayed it more dipper whan you
sayd you wolde warne me of al euelles that you hulde hire of me, for if your grace
had not a good opinion of me you wolde not haue offered frindeship to me that
way, that al men iuge the contrarye, but what may I more say, thanke God for pro=
uidinge suche frendes to me, desiringe God to enriche me with ther longe life, and
me grace to be in hart no les thankeful to receyue it, than I nowe am glad in wri=
tinge to shewe it. and althongh I haue plentye of matter, hire I wil staye, for I
knowe you ar not quiet to rede . Frome Cheston this present saterday .

Although I could not be plentiful in giving thanks for the manifold kindness received
at your Highness' hand at my departure, yet I am some things to be born withal, for
truly I was replete with sorrow to depart from your Highness, especially leaving you
undoubtful of health, and albeit I answered little, I weighed it more deeper when you
said you would warn me of all evils that you should hear of me, for if your grace
had not a good opinion of me you would not have offered friendship to me that
way, that all men judge the contrary, but what may I more say than thank God for providing such friends to me, desiring God to enrich me with their long life, and
me grace to be in heart no less thankful to receive it, than I now am glad in writing to show it, and although I have plenty of matter, here I will stay for I
know you are not quiet to read. From Cheston this present Saturday.

Your highness' humble daughter

Elizabeth

Reassurance from a cast-off bride
Letter from Anne of Cleves to her brother

21 JULY 1540

The fact that Henry VIII put aside his fourth wife, Anne of Cleves, is well known, yet this letter, written from Anne to her brother, Wilhelm, Duke of Jülich-Cleves (two former territories that are now part of the northern region of modern Germany and the Netherlands), sheds more light on the circumstances surrounding this peculiar situation. It was written in July 1540, shortly after the judgement was produced by the Convocations of Canterbury and York that declared the nullity of Anne's marriage to the King.

In her childhood, Anne had been betrothed to François, heir to the duchy of Lorraine. However, this unofficial betrothal did not result in a formal marriage alliance, so Anne was put forward as a potential bride for Henry VIII in the late 1530s, in response to the contemporary political situation. Henry moved to ally himself with Cleves following his excommunication by Pope Paul III and after a defensive alliance had been formed by two key European rulers: François I of France and the Holy Roman Emperor, Charles V. The lands owned by Anne's father, Duke Johann (Duke of Jülich-Cleves 1490–1539), were strategically significant and her brother, Wilhelm, was recognised as Duke of Guelders (an historical duchy in the Low Countries) in 1538, which gave the territory coastal access – the importance of which would not have gone unnoticed by Charles V in the event of potential future conflict.

Duke Johann died in early 1539, leaving Wilhelm to deal with the marriage negotiations. Wilhelm was keen to promote a match and welcomed envoys from England to report on the suitability of a marriage. After Henry had settled on Anne, the government of Cleves assured him that the previous betrothal had not led to a binding marriage contract.

The pair duly wed, though Henry was unable to consummate his marriage to Anne – he was suffering from some form of sexual dysfunction at this time, which he ascribed to fears that the marriage was invalid as a result of Anne's previous betrothal. Anne, however, confirms her virginity in the letter: 'my Body remaineth in the integrity which I brought into this Realm.'

By this time the political situation had changed, making the need for an alliance with Cleves less pressing and, what's more, Henry had fallen in love with one of the Queen's ladies-in-waiting, Catherine Howard. An ecclesiastical inquiry into the validity of the marriage was thereby called and although initially Anne refused to consent, she did eventually agree to the annulment.

Anne received a handsome settlement that also, as highlighted by the letter, defined her relationship with the King as that of brother and sister, although the settlement stipulated that her future communications with Cleves would be monitored. This Anne accepted reluctantly but it might explain the accepting tone of her situation in the letter and also her attempts to pacify Wilhelm, who she implied in the letter was displeased with the situation. Anne was in a precarious position, but in order to safeguard her settlement, it was important that she complied with Henry's wishes.

The seals of Anne of Cleves, 9 July 1540.

My dere and welbeloved Brother, After my most
hartie Comendacons, where by yor L^{res} of the 13.th of
this Month. wch I have seen written to the Kings Ma:^{ty}
of England, my most dere and most kinde Brother I
doe p^{er}ceive, that yo^w take the Matter lately moved &
determined between him and me, sore what to heart
ffor as much as I had rather yo^w knew the truth by mine
Advertisem^t. then for want thereof yr should be deceived
by bad Reports, I thought meete to write these p^{re}sent
L^{res} unto yo^w by the which it shall please yo^w to understand
that being Substantially Advertised, how the Nobles &
Comens of this Realme dessired the Kings Ma:^{ty} to comitte y^e
Examination of the Matter of Marriage between his highnesse &
me to the Examination and determination of the whole Clergie
of this Realme, I did then willing consent thereunto, And since
the Determination made have also upon Intimation of their
proceedings allowed, approved and agreed unto, the same
wherein I had more respect (as beseemed me) to truth then
to any worldly affection that might move me to the Contrary
And did the rather Condescend thereunto, for that my Body
remaineth in the integritie which I brought into this
Realme. And being the matter thus signified, to advor-
-tise yo^w how I am used, Surely the Kings Highnesse
whom I cannot now justly have, he will repute as my
husband, hath nevertheless taken and adopted me for
his Sister, and as a most kinde loveing and friendly Broth^r
useth me wth as much or more humanitie, and Liberalitie,
as yo^w I myselfe, or any of our Kinne or Allye, could well

with or desire, where w.th I (am) p...y for mine own parte
so well satisfied, that I much desire, that my good Mother
and you should know this my State & condicon, not doubt-
but when yo.u shall throughly wage all things yo.u woll s...
use yo.r selfe towards this Noble and good Prince, as he
may continue his ffriendshippe towards yo.u w.ch on his
Highnesse behalfe shall nothing be Impaired or allered
for this Matter, unlesse the fault should be in yo.r selfe, where
=of I would be most sorry; for so it hath pleased his highn...
to signifie unto me, which I have thought necessary to writ
unto yo.u And also that God willing I propose to leade
my Life in this Realme, haveing his Grace so good Lord
as he is towards me, lest for want of true knowledge of
my Minde and Condicon ye might otherwise take this
Matter then ye ought, and in other sort cared for me th...
ye have cause, Thus &c.

Anna Duchesse borne of
Cleveses Gelike Gelder et
Berge, yo.r Loveing Sister.

21 July 1540

My dear and well-beloved Brother. After my most
hearty commendations, whereby your letters of the 13th of
this month, which I have seen written to the King's Majesty
of England, my most dear and most kind Brother I
do perceive that you take the Matter lately moved and
determined between him and me somewhat to heart
for as much I had rather you knew the truth by mine
advertisement than forward thereof you should be deceived
by vain Reports. I thought meet to write these present
letters unto you by the which it shall please you to understand
that being substantially advertised, how the Nobles and
Commons of this Realm desired the King's Majesty to commit the
examination of the matter of marriage between his highness and
me to the examination and determination of the whole clergy
of this realm. I did then willing consent thereunto. And since
the determination made have also upon intimation of their
proceedings allowed, approved and agreed unto, the same
wherein I had more respect (as beseemed me) to truth than
to any worldly affection that might move me to the contrary.
And did the neither condescend thereunto, for that my Body
remaineth in the integrity which I brought into this
Realm. And being the matter signified, to advertise you how I am thus used. Surely the King's Highness
whom I can not now justly have me well repute as my

husband, hath nevertheless taken and adopted me for

his sister, and as a most kind, loving and friendly Brother

useth me with as much or more humanity and liberality

as you. I myself or any of our kin or all you could well

wish or desire, where with I am for mine own part

so well satisfied that I much desire that my good Mother

and you should know this my state and condition, not doubt

but when you shall thoroughly weigh all things you will so

use yourself towards this Noble and good Prince, as he

may continue his Friendship towards you which on his

Highness' behalf shall nothing be impaired or altered.

for this matter, unless the fault should be in yourself, where-

of I would be most sorry; for so it hath pleased his highness

to signify unto me, which I have thought necessary to write

unto you. And also that God willing I propose to lead

my life in this realm, having his Grace so good Lord

as he is towards me, lest for want of true knowledge of

my mind and condition you might otherwise take this

matter than you ought, and in other sort care for me then

you have cause. Thus yours

                                        Anna Duchess born of
                                        Cleves Gallic Guelder and
                                        Berger your loving Sister

One last love letter
The final letter from the Earl of Leicester to Queen Elizabeth I

29 AUGUST 1588

When Elizabeth I died, her bedside casket contained her special personal treasures, among which was a document inscribed 'his last letter' that she had received from Robert Dudley, Earl of Leicester. The letter itself says little of import but its preservation and the inscription bear testimony to one of the greatest love affairs of all time.

Elizabeth and Robert had been close since childhood. They shared a tutor in Roger Ascham. Later, after the plot to put Jane Grey on the throne, when Robert was imprisoned in the Tower, his stay overlapped with that of Elizabeth, who was suspected of plotting against her sister, Mary. They were intelligent, charismatic and overwhelmingly ambitious individuals who shared a love of hunting, music and conversation. In another world or another time they would have been made for each other. Elizabeth was not, however, a woman to think the world well lost for love and she knew Dudley was vain, arrogant and ambitious (faults she possessed herself) and that England would never accept him as king.

Nevertheless, the two remained close: he had mortgaged his estates to lend her money when she needed it and nearly bankrupted himself building a special garden and elaborate entertainments for her visit to his home in Kenilworth, reputedly creating a second garden overnight when she pettishly complained she could not see the original from her room. In return, her marks of favour towards him provoked comment throughout Europe, and she wrote to him often, signing 'As you know, ever the same. ER'.

A manuscript illustration of Elizabeth I in 1584.

Aware that marriage was not on the cards, Robert was not one to pine alone and he was married twice: first to Amy Robsart, whose death in mysterious circumstances caused a scandal; and eighteen years later to the Queen's cousin Lettice Knollys – an unauthorised match that angered the Queen. She eventually forgave him and they remained close for the rest of his life. She herself never married, instead playing a complicated game of matrimonial politics among the royal houses of Europe and ending as the emblematic Virgin Queen.

The letter itself is short and formal. It is no outpouring of youthful passion, but this makes it all the more poignant: it is a letter between two old friends, both ageing and in increasingly poor health. A letter written to a woman who once stated 'a thousand eyes see all I do' is perforce a letter carefully crafted. Elizabeth called him 'eyes' and they used the device 'öö' in their letters to allude to this. Here, the device can be seen above the word 'poor'. She has sent him medicine and, as the postscript indicates, a recent token. He sends his thanks, noting he is at Rycote in Oxfordshire – a mansion she knew and that they had visited together. There is significant subtext here.

Dudley's last letter is a moving document. Whether or not Elizabeth and Leicester were lovers in a sexual sense is a matter for historical conjecture, but what this letter is undoubtedly testament to is a forty-year relationship – possibly Elizabeth's closest. He died a few days after writing it. At the time this was attributed to malaria, although later historians have suggested he may have been suffering from stomach cancer. When Elizabeth was told of his death she locked herself in her room for three days, and went on to keep this last letter in her close personal effects until her own death fifteen years later, in 1603.

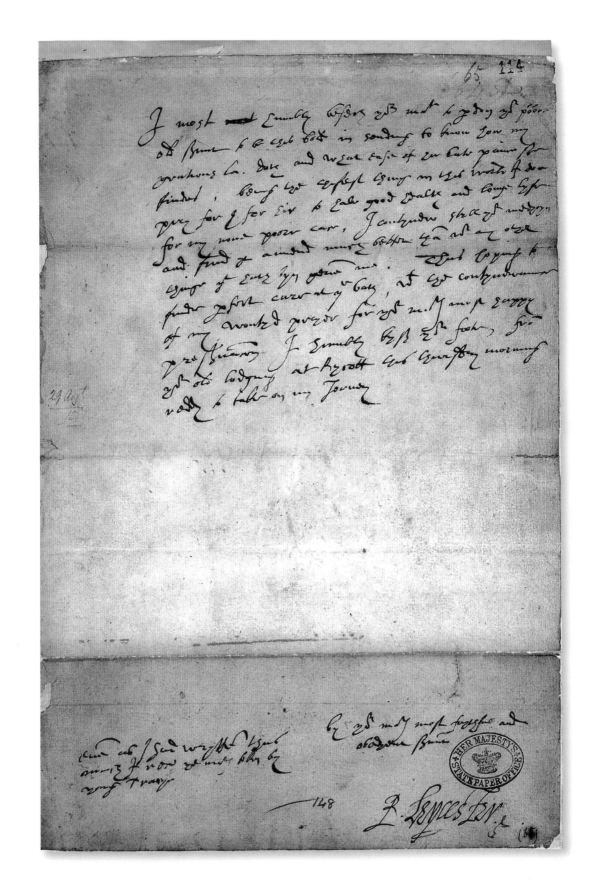

I most humbly besech god mat to gyve yo pooer
old frind to C that be ys sending to know how you my
gracyous la. dothe and what ease of ewe late payn ys
fynded, beyng the cheffest thyng in thes world I do
pray for E for hir to have good healthe and long lyff
for my none poor cace, I contynew styll yt medycyn
and fynd yt amends muche better the at my cume
cume yf can by youe me. Thus hopyng to
fynd yfort cure at yo bath, wt the continuance
of my wontyd prayr for yt meste deere
[ ] I humbly kiss yt foote, fro
yor old lodgyng at hygatt thys thursday mornyng
redy to take on my Jorney

dene wt I had wrytst thus
amu I rece yo mats letter by
wery trewy

by yor mats most fayttfull and
obedyent serva

148

R: Leycester

I most humbly beseech your Majesty to pardon your poor
old servant to be thus bold in sending to know how my
gracious lady doth, and what ease of her late pain she
finds, being the chiefest thing in the world I do pray
for, for her to have good health and long life. For my
own poor case, I continue still your medicine and find
that [it] amends much better than any other thing that
hath been given me. Thus hoping to find perfect cure
at the bath, with the continuance of my wonted prayer
for your Majesty's most happy preservation, I humbly
kiss your foot. From your old lodging at Rycote, this
Thursday morning, ready to take on my Journey, by Your
Majesty's most faithful and obedient servant,

Even as I had writ thus much, I
received Your Majesty's token by
Young Tracey.

                    R. Leicester

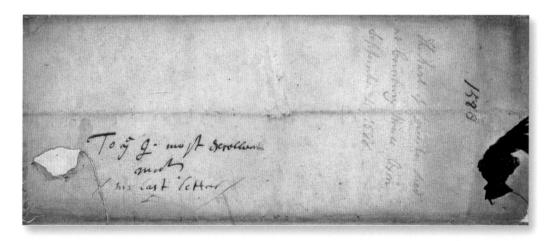

"His last letter"

News from home
Letter from Lily Wilde to the governor of Reading Gaol

1897

The Marquis of Queensbury assembled an array of witnesses in his defence and the prosecution case collapsed. On 5 April 1895, Oscar Wilde was arrested and charged with gross indecency. The evidence from the libel case against Queensbury was turned around and used against Wilde. He was convicted at the Central Criminal Court and sentenced to two years in prison with hard labour.

On 18 February 1895, at the Albermarle Club in Piccadilly, John Sholto Douglas, Marquis of Queensbury, handed a card to the hall porter. The hall porter passed the card to its intended recipient. The card bore a short message, that, although open to some interpretation due to the handwriting, is generally considered to read: 'For Oscar Wilde, posing sodomite'. This led Oscar Wilde to bring a libel case against Queensbury, who was the father of Wilde's lover, Lord Alfred Bruce Douglas.

The case was heard in March 1895. The Marquis of Queensbury assembled an array of witnesses in his defence and the prosecution case collapsed. On 5 April 1895, Oscar Wilde was arrested and charged with gross indecency. The evidence from the libel case against Queensbury was turned around and used against Wilde. He was convicted at the Central Criminal Court and sentenced to two years in prison with hard labour.

During this period, many letters were sent to the governor of Reading Gaol by Oscar Wilde's friends, his relatives, and by complete strangers. The content of these letters ranges from friends requesting permission to visit him to deal with his affairs to members of the public offering support and, in some cases, gifts.

This letter to the prison governor from Wilde's sister-in-law, Lily Wilde, is particularly interesting and touching. Beginning with the rather strange request to return his brother's waistcoat, it ends with the poignant plea to pass on her love to Oscar, along with a message regarding the health of his mother. We can have no idea whether Wilde saw this letter or knew of it or its contents, yet it seems unlikely as the letter was sent to the governor and not to Wilde. We also don't know whether the waistcoat was returned as requested.

The collection of The National Archives holds other key records of this famous case, including the card that was handed to the hall porter at the Albemarle Club. In July 1896, Oscar Wilde made a petition from his cell in Reading jail to the Home Secretary for early release. The petition is also held in The National Archives and gives a stark account of Oscar Wilde's time in gaol and to the solitary confinement to which he was subjected. He was bankrupt, suffering failing health, and clearly at the limit of what he could bear. However impassioned this petition, though, it failed: Oscar Wilde remained in jail for almost another year, completing the entirety of his sentence. Following his release in 1897 he left for France, where he died in 1900.

Oscar Wilde, prior to his imprisonment.

146 Oakley St
Chelsea
Monday

Dear Sir

My brother in law
Mr Oscar Wilde on
the day of the verdict
took ~more~ his brother's
Waistcoat in place
of his own. Would
you be so kind as
to send it to me

& I will forward
the right one. I do
not know if you
would extend yr
kindness to give
a small message
from me but as
I am expecting
my confinement
shortly & one's life
is always more or

51

lies in danger perhaps
you would relax
the rule. If so would
you give him my
fondest love & say
how often I think
of him & long to
see him: also what
perhaps will give
him the most pleasure
that his Mother
is wonderfully well

& came down to
my bedroom Sunday
week. That I have
heard absolutely
nothing of his Wife
or children since he
was here so that I
presume indeed I
heard from Mr Russell
that she is thinking
of following the advice
of Sir George Lewis.
I hope you will
not think it wrong
of me to ask you

52

what I have, but
Mr Haldane who
I have seen told me
you were very kind
to my unhappy
brother in law.

very truly yrs
Lily Wilde

146 Oakley St

Chelsea

Monday

Dear Sir

My brother in law Mr Oscar Wilde on the
day of the verdict wore his brother's waistcoat
in place of his own. Would you be so kind as to
send it to me. I will forward the right one. I
do not know if you would extend your kindness
to give a small message from me but as I am
expecting my confinement shortly & one's life
is always more or less in danger perhaps you
would relax the rule. If so would you give him
my fondest love and say how often I think of
him & long to see him: also what perhaps will
give him the most pleasure that his Mother is
wonderfully well & came down to my bedroom
Sunday week. That I have heard absolutely
nothing of his Wife or children since he was
here so that I presume indeed I heard from Mr
Russell that she is thinking of following the
advice of Sir George Lewis. I hope you will not
think it wrong of me to ask you what I have,
but Mr Haldane who I have seen told me you were
very kind to my unhappy brother in law.

Very truly yrs

Lily Wilde

Enforced emigration to Canada
A father's desperate letter to Stepney Barnardo's children's home

20 JANUARY 1911

This letter was written in response to a letter Rowe had received from Barnardo's children's home in Stepney informing him that his daughters, Hilda Kate and Eva May (aged twelve and sixteen respectively), were likely to be selected to go with the next party of children to Canada, where they would be received into a Canadian family provided they 'behaved well'.

Both girls had been resident in the Dr Barnardo's Girls' Village Home, Barkingside, Ilford, since 1907 when they were committed at the Petty Sessional Court in Southampton, under the Prevention of Cruelty to Children Act 1904. Court documents note that their mother had died in November 1905 and that their father, a painter, was said to be of 'lazy and drunken habits'. In March 1906 he was sentenced to three months' hard labour for having neglected his children. The neglect, however, was subsequently resumed upon his release, and in November 1907 he was sentenced to a further six months' hard labour for repeating the crime – the children, who had undergone 'the severest privations', having been found to be living 'under the most wretched conditions and in a state bordering on starvation'.

This case was typical of many of those of children who were sent overseas at the beginning of the twentieth century, although British child-emigration schemes had been in operation since as early as 1618 and continued as late as 1967. During this period it is estimated that some 150,000 children were sent to the British Colonies and Dominions, most notably America, Australia and Canada, but also Rhodesia and New Zealand. Many of the children were in the care of the voluntary organisations that arranged for their migration. Child emigration peaked from the 1870s until 1914, and some 80,000 children were sent to Canada alone during this period.

Mid-nineteenth century Victorian Britain did not smile upon the poor – and the big cities were full of them. Those who swelled the slums were people who had flocked to the industrialised cities from the country in search of jobs in factories and the docks. Many were Irish refugees from the Potato Famine of 1845–1849, and all of them struggled to eke out a marginal existence. Food was scarce, sickness and epidemics of cholera and smallpox were rife and housing grew more and more scarce. In the 1860s, houses were demolished to make way for the railways and new ones were not within the reach of the poor. By the 1880s, the housing shortage had become chronic, with more and more people crowding into the tenements and slum landlords making huge profits. Crime and lawlessness flourished, and in this hostile environment poor children grew up with little food, no education, sometimes abandoned by their parents and often exploited for their work.

Into the morass stepped several philanthropists, most of them imbued with an evangelical mission to spread the word of God and rescue the poor from sin. They set to work with energy and dedication, establishing shelters for the destitute, and schools and homes for their young. However, the stream of those in need was never-ending and with the rise of unemployment in the late 1860s, the charities and the Poor Law Unions began to send people to Canada, freeing up space in the workhouse for more people.

Dr Barnardo was probably the biggest player in child-migration schemes in the nineteenth and twentieth centuries, with the result that by the early 1900s Canadians were calling all child emigrants, no matter where they originated, 'Barnardo boys'. By the time of his death in September 1905 nearly 16,000 children had been sent by him to Canada, according to an article reporting on his funeral in the *Illustrated London News*. In fact, the true figure was 18,172. Furthermore, by 1939 more than 30,000 children had been sent to Canada by his organisation.

The aim of child migration was often to increase the population within the Colonies, and to improve labour and productivity there. Although most schemes were presented as being for the benefit and welfare of the child, few actually took the feelings of the children into account.

Sadly, it would seem that the Rowe girls never managed to see their father again after they departed Southampton for Quebec in Canada on board the SS *Sicilian*, on 29 June 1911, with more than 150 other children from Dr Barnardo's homes – all destined for homes in Peterborough, Ontario.

203442

Copy

18 to 26, Stepney Causeway,

London, E.

20th January 1911.

To Mr G. Rowe,

I am desired by the Managers of these Institutions to inform you that your daughters , Eva May and Hilda Kate Rowe, now in the Girls' Village Home, Barkingside, Ilford, will probably be selected to go with the next Party of children to our Branch Home in Canada, from which place they will, if they behave well, be received into a Canadian family and find a happy home.

Should you desire to write to the children, their address is - c/o The Secretary, Margaret Cox Girls' Home, Peterboro', Ontario, Canada. Your letters will only need a penny stamp if they do not exceed an ounce in weight

The Managers will be pleased to furnish you at intervals with tidings of their progress and welfare in the new country.

I am directed to inform you that in Canada they will be under the same kind and watchful supervision, on the part of experienced ladies belonging to our Home, as they would have enjoyed had they remained in England. The Managers have every reason to believe that their best interests will be secured by their emigration.

I am,

Yours faithfully,

(Signed)   George Code

Honorary Secretary

371 Parsand Rd
Southampton

Sir   23 JAN 1911   203442   Jan 22
Ackd
23/1/11

I was surprised to
receive a letter from you
telling me you were
sending my two little girls
to Canada   which I do
not approve of   and if
there any means of stopping
it I shall do so = I think
they are quite far enough
a way from me now

I called on your
Manager at the Southampton
Branch on Saturday and
he told me when their
time was up they
would be left there
and that means to say
I shall never see the
Children again I consider
my self I have been
punished quite enough

I shall never be able the

to save the money for
them to come back
I cannot pay my way
now work being so
very slack   I shall
endeavour to see the
Magistrates who made the
order.   I think it is
most cruel for two
Children to be sent
so far away from
there Father & Friends that
loves them so dear

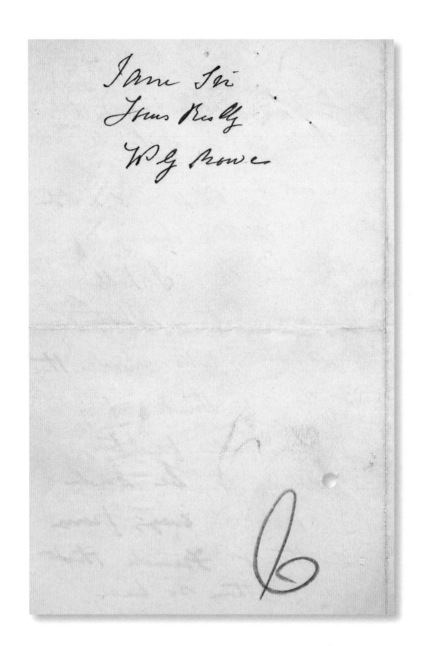

371 Parkwood Road
Southampton
Jan 22 [1911]

Sir

        I was surprised to receive a letter
from you telling me you were sending my
little girls to Canada which I do not approve
of and if there [are] any means of stopping
it I shall do so. I think they are quite
[sic] far enough away from me now. I called
on your manager at the Southampton Branch on
Saturday and he told me when there [sic] time
was up they would be left there and that
means to say I shall never see the children
again. I consider myself I have been punished
quite enough.

        I shall never be able to save the
money for them to come back. I cannot pay
my way now work being so very slack. I shall
endeavour to see the Magistrates who made the
order. I think it is most cruel to be sent so
far away from there [sic] father and friends
that loves them so dear.

        I am Sir
         Yours truly
         W G Rowe

'An outrage of Christian principles'
An unexpurgated publication of *Lady Chatterley's Lover*

5 NOVEMBER 1960

Despite having been published in its entirety in countries around the world since the 1920s, by 1960 only the expurgated version of *Lady Chatterley's Lover* – known as *The First Lady Chatterley* – by DH Lawrence was available to buy in the United Kingdom.

Describing the affair between a woman and her husband's gamekeeper, the theme, descriptions and language of the full version of the book were still considered by some to be shocking at the beginning of the 1960s.

Following revisions to the Obscene Publications Act in 1959, however, Penguin Books Limited took the decision to publish the unexpurgated version of the book in the UK. They printed 200,000 copies, which they proposed to retail at 3s 6d – a very affordable price. This bold move led to the famous trial. Charged with publishing an 'Obscene Article', the trial of Penguin Books took place at the Old Bailey between 20 October and 2 November 1960.

The Obscene Publications Act 1959 deemed a book to be obscene if it could be proved that its content could tend to deprave and corrupt readers. It would not be deemed to be an obscene publication if it were justified as being for the public good on the grounds that it was in the interests of science, literature, art or learning. In this case, the prosecution based its argument on the opinion that *Lady Chatterley's Lover* was obscene and could corrupt and deprave. The defence argued that it was a work of art justified as being for the public good, and called thirty-five witnesses – including famous authors and academics – to testify to the artistic and moral value of the book. The prosecution called no witnesses. After hearing all of the arguments and deliberating for three hours, the jury returned a unanimous verdict of not guilty. Penguin Books went on to publish *Lady Chatterley's Lover* in full; all 200,000 copies sold out on the first day.

The collection of The National Archives contains the papers of the prosecution – the papers of the Director of Public Prosecutions. This includes preparatory papers and notes, the full transcript of the trial, and meticulously underlined copies of the books, highlighting specific passages of a sexual nature.

Sir Allen Lane, the managing director of Penguin Books, with a copy of *Lady Chatterley's Lover*.

As well as the official records of the prosecution, The National Archives has many letters from members of the public, horrified at the outcome of the trial and the 'threats' posed to society by the publication. These were handled by the Home Office and many were addressed to the Home Secretary. However, this example shows that some were not satisfied with merely contacting a politician and instead appealed directly to the Queen, imploring her to intervene so that the decision might be overturned.

The majority of these letters deal with the fear of moral corruption and give a fascinating insight into the opinions of some quarters of the public at that time, as well as raising an interesting question of how much opinions on the nature of morality and taste have moved on since 1960.

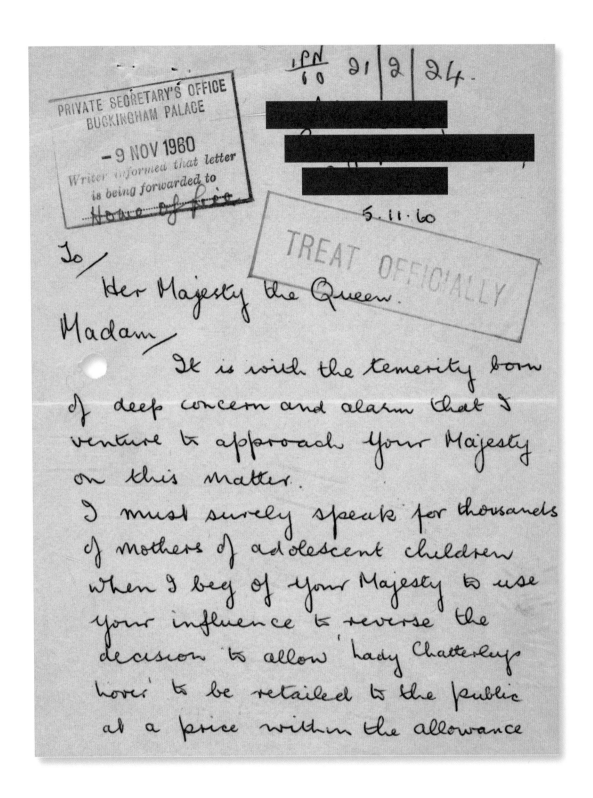

IPN
10   21/2/24.

5.11.60

TREAT OFFICIALLY

To/
  Her Majesty the Queen.

Madam/
        It is with the temerity born
of deep concern and alarm that I
venture to approach Your Majesty
on this matter.
I must surely speak for thousands
of mothers of adolescent children
when I beg of Your Majesty to use
your influence to reverse the
decision to allow 'Lady Chatterley's
lover' to be retailed to the public
at a price within the allowance

of youths and girls still at school. The depravity of this book is unspeakable, and with your sheltered upbringing in a Christian home Your Majesty cannot conceive the immoral situations which will be put before innocent minds.

Many a girl, who, reading out of a desire to be up-to-date, will have her approach to marriage warped, and boys of the age of your son, the Prince of Wales, and mine a year older, may learn such things from school fellows that will refute the sanctity of the body, and turn healthy inquiring minds to furtive, lewd and immoral pursuits.

I do beg of Your Majesty and Prince Philip to make your wishes on the subject public, and so shame those who are responsible for this outrage of Christian principles, that a change of legislation will be brought about before it is too late.

I remain,

Your Majesty's faithful and dutiful servant,

H.O. WHITEHALL
11 NOV 1960
GEN. REGISTER

Address redacted

5.11.60

To

      Her Majesty the Queen

Madam,

     It is with temerity born of deep concern and alarm that I venture to approach your Majesty on this matter.

     I must surely speak for thousands of mothers of adolescent children when I beg of your Majesty to use your influence to reverse the decision to allow 'Lady Chatterleys Lover' to be retailed to the public at a price within the allowance of youths and girls still at school.

     The depravity of this book is unspeakable, and with your sheltered upbringing in a Christian home Your Majesty cannot conceive the immoral situations which will be put before innocent minds. Many a girl, who, reading out of a desire to be up-to-date, will have her approach to marriage warped, and boys of the age of your son, the Prince of Wales, and mine, a year older, may learn such things from school fellows that well refute the sanctity of the body, and turn healthy inquiring minds to furtive, lewd and immoral pursuits.

     I do beg of Your Majesty and Prince Philip to make your wishes on the subject public, and so shame those who are responsible for his outrage of Christian principles, that a change of legislation will be brought about before it is too late.

    I remain,

     Your Majesty's faithful
       and dutiful servant,

       Name redacted

Time to make up one's mind
Princess Margaret's marriage correspondence

SUMMER 1955

Royal marriages can be a time for national celebration, with street parties bringing communities together, families crowding around television screens, and flags fluttering between street lamps. They can also cause great upheaval and crises that strike to the very core of Britain's constitutional monarchy. Edward VIII's marriage to the American divorcee Wallis Simpson is a case in point, since it forced the abdication of the young king in 1936. Seventeen years later, his niece Princess Margaret also found herself in an unfortunate position – in the eyes of the British establishment – when it came to falling in love.

Group Captain Peter Townsend, an RAF flying ace who led a squadron of Hawker Hurricane pilots throughout the Battle of Britain, had been made comptroller of the Queen Mother's restructured staff at Clarence House following the death of George VI. Townsend had previously served as equerry to the king and by April 1953 the thirty-eight-year-old father-of-two had divorced his wife and proposed to the twenty-two-year-old princess.

Once again the Church of England's opposition to divorce was a barrier, as were the views of Winston Churchill's Conservative government. In addition, Queen Elizabeth II's consent was required under the Royal Marriages Act of 1772. The situation was further complicated by the fact that Margaret's sister had yet to be crowned, with the coronation being organised for June. Indeed, it was at the coronation at Westminster Abbey that the relationship became public in somewhat subtle circumstances: Margaret was seen brushing some fluff off Townsend's uniform as she waited for her carriage.

By the summer of 1955 Anthony Eden was prime minister – himself having divorced and remarried – and studies were underway to determine whether an Act of Parliament could eliminate the need for the Queen to give permission for the marriage if Margaret, and her future children, were to be removed from the line of succession. For her part, the Queen was reportedly supportive of the proposal.

Above and right: Princess Margaret with Peter Townsend.

On 15 August Margaret wrote to Eden from Balmoral Castle, acutely aware of the growing intensity in press speculation as she approached her twenty-fifth birthday. She assured the prime minister she would not see Townsend until she returned to London in October. Townsend would then be taking his annual leave and Margaret wrote that she had to see him in this period as: 'It is only by seeing him in this way that I feel I can properly decide whether I can marry him or not.' Margaret saw the decision as hers to make rather than anybody else's, and informed Eden of this in clear terms. However, she was also 'particularly anxious that whatever may happen, may not cause any embarrassment to you personally, or to the government'.

In the end, Margaret called off the engagement on 31 October, citing her overriding duty to the Commonwealth and to the teachings of the Church. In May 1960 her marriage at Westminster Abbey to photographer Antony Armstrong-Jones, later Earl of Snowdon, was the first royal wedding to be televised. The couple's social circle included many of the stars of the 1960s and provided plenty of copy for tabloid headline writers before the pair separated in 1978.

10, Downing Street,
Whitehall.

David

<u>Princess Margaret</u>

The P.M. spoke to Sir N. Brook this morning & discussed the situation. He said he thought it cd. do the monarchy no good if the decision were held up much longer. Sir N. Brook agreed & suggested that the Palace might

×/ put it out (most informally) that the Princess must herself be given time to make up her mind. They agreed that nothing shd. be said to Cabinet yet though the P.M. might mention the matter to the intimates before the Audience on Tuesday.

The P.M. then spoke to Sir M. Adeane, who agreed to consider ×/. He said The Queen had done all

...ing a decision easier.
...op of C. had said to him
...like to see the A/bp. The
...t the Princess shd. go
...that the A/bp shd. go
...(rather this interview
...in the week.

...ill consider mentioning
to the Queen on Tuesday that harm will be done if there is much more delay, & even possibly offering to see the Princess himself to say so. Meanwhile I gathered from the conversation between the P.M & Adeane that the P.M. will not talk to Ministers (ie. not even the intimates) before Tuesday pm. I will try to confirm this.

M.

23/X

<u>David</u>

Princess Margaret

The P.M. spoke to Sir N Brook this morning &
discussed the situation. He said he thought it cd.
do the monarchy no good if the decision were held up
much longer. Sir N. Brook agreed and requested that
the Palace might put it out (most informally) that the
princess must herself be given time to make up her
mind. They agreed that nothing shd be said in Cabinet
yet though the P.M. might mention the matter to the
intimates before the Audience on Tuesday.

The P.M. thus spoke to Sir M. Adeane, who agreed
to consider. He said The Queen had done all that was
possible to bring a decision nearer. The P.M. said the
Archbishop of C[anterbury] had said to him that the
Princess wd. like to see the A/bp. The P.M. had advised
that the Princess shd. go to Lambeth rather than
that the A/bp shd go to Clarence House. I gather this
interview will take place later in the week.

I think the P.M. will consider mentioning to the
Queen on Thursday that harm will be done if there is
much more delay, & and even possibly offering to see the
Princess himself to say so. Meanwhile I gathered from
the conversation between the P.M. & Adeane that the P.M.
will not talk to Ministers (ie not even the intimates)
before Tuesday pm. I will try to confirm this.

The prolongation of uncertainty, with continuing Press interest, discussion and comment, is doing some harm. It is not good for the Queen and the Royal Family. Nor is it good for the Princess. Everyone has been anxious that she should be free to reach her own decision, and the attitude of the Queen and Government has been matched by the mood of the country. But that mood could change to one containing some elements of boredom and exasperation, and this would not be good whatever the decis...

What her decision should ...
it is easy to ~~press~~ ~~any~~ opinio...
Princess know what the true s...
can be and whether she is ab...
whole happiness lies in going ah...
can weigh for herself the argu...
to go ahead with it the course...
renunciation of rights of succe...
Commonwealth Government ha...

succession and on the Royal Marriage Act

If she is uncertain in her mind, she will doubtless weigh carefully all the adverse considerations, which should then assume greater force. It is clear that it is not a marriage which all sections of the country would welcome wholeheartedly. ~~The Princess is very near to the Queen who is Head of the Church.~~ Anyone in a public position must take these considerations into account. They apply with special force to the Princess, sister to the Queen who is Head of the Church. The marriage cannot but ~~do some harm~~, though not of course fatal harm, and not necessarily lasting harm to the Royal Family, even though the Princess recognises the situation by ~~renouncing~~ the succession. ~~Their in itself though~~ it would be necessary in the circumstances, this in itself ~~was~~ is not good for the Crown. And there is also the point of view mentioned in today's Times, that the Princess, if she decides to marry, will thereby ~~need to~~ retire into private life. It is clear that the degree to which she could carry out representative functions would depend on public opinion.

The prolongation of uncertainty, with continuing Press interest, discussion and comment, is doing some harm. It is not good for the Queen and the Royal Family. Nor is it good for the Princess. Everyone has been anxious that she should be free to reach her own decision and the attitude of the Queen and Government has been matched by the mood of the country. But that mood could change to one containing some elements of boredom and exasperation, and this would not be good whatever the decision.

What her decision should be is not a matter on which it is easy to express my opinion. How can anyone but the Princess know what the true state of her feelings towards T can be and whether she is absolutely convinced that her whole happiness lies in going ahead with this marriage. She can weigh for herself the arguments against. If she decides to go ahead with it the course of action is pretty clear: renunciation of rights of succession: consultation with Commonwealth Government leading to legislation on the succession and on the Royal Marriage Act.

If she is uncertain in her mind she will doubtless weigh carefully all the adverse considerations, which should then assume greater force. It is clear that it is not a marriage which all sections of the country would welcome wholeheartedly. Anyone in a public position must take these considerations into account. They apply with special force to the Princess, sister to the Queen who is Head of the Church. The marriage cannot but do some harm, though not of course fatal harm, and not necessarily lasting harm, to the Royal Family, even though the Princess recognises the situation by renouncing the succession. Though it would be necessary in the circumstances, this in itself is not good for the Crown. And there is also the point of view mentioned in today's Times, that the Princess, if she decides to marry, will thereby retire into private life. It is clear that the degree to which she could carry out representative functions would depend on public opinion.

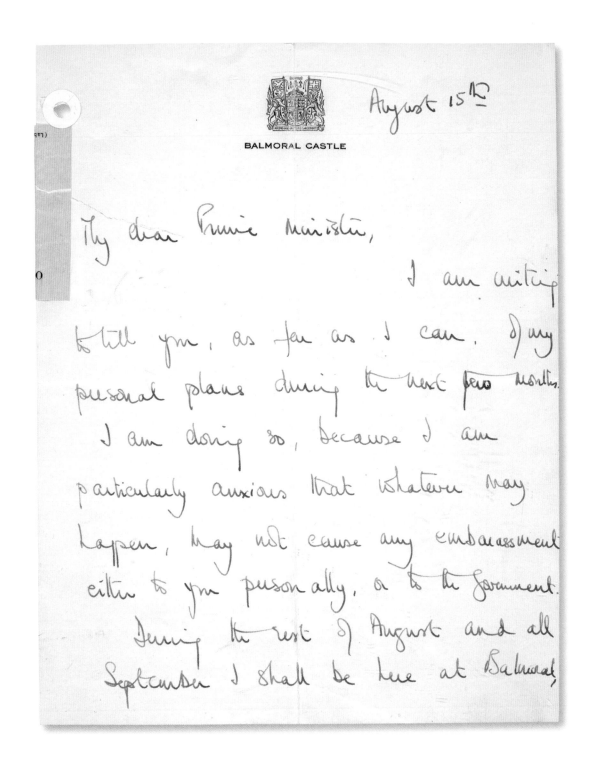

August 15th

BALMORAL CASTLE

My dear Prime Minister,

I am writing to tell you, as far as I can, of my personal plans during the next few months.

I am doing so, because I am particularly anxious that whatever may happen, may not cause any embarrassment either to you personally, or to the Government.

During the rest of August and all September I shall be here at Balmoral,

and I have no doubt that during
this time - especially on my birthday
on August 21st - the press will encourage
every sort of speculation about the
possibility of my marrying Group Captain
Peter Townsend -

I am not going to see him
during this time, but in October
I shall be returning to London, and
he will then be taking his annual
leave - I do certainly hope to see him

BALMORAL CASTLE

while he is there, although I well
know this will provoke the press to
still further enquiries & guesses.

But, it is only by seeing him
in this way that I feel I can
properly decide whether I can marry
him or not.

At the end of October or early
November I very much hope to be
in a position to tell you and
the other commonwealth Prime Ministers

what I intend to do.

(The Queen of course knows I am
writing to you about this, but of
course no one else does, and as
everything is so uncertain I know you
will regard it entirely as a confidence.

Yours very sincerely

Margaret

My Dear Prime Minister,

I am writing to tell you, as far as I can, of my personal plans during the next few months.

I am doing so because I am particularly anxious that whatever may happen, may not cause any embarrassment either to you personally, or to the Government.

During the rest of August and all September I shall be here at Balmoral and I have no doubt that during this time — especially on my birthday on August 21st — the press will encompass every sort of speculation about the possibility of my marrying Group Captain Peter Townsend.

I am not going to see him during this time but in October I shall be returning to London, and he will then be taking his annual leave — I do certainly hope to see him while he is there, although I well know this will provoke the press to still further enquiries & guesses.

But, it is only by seeing him in this way that I feel I can properly decide whether I can marry him or not.

At the end of October or early November I very much hope to be in a position to tell you and the other commonwealth Prime Ministers what I intend to do.

The Queen of course knows I am writing to you about this, but of course no one else does, and as everything is so uncertain I know you will regard it entirely as a confidence.

Yours very sincerely

Margaret

Art, science and
popular culture

Celebrity spotting in eighteenth-century Venice
Elizeus Burges to Thomas Pelham-Holles

20 JANUARY 1730

Elizeus Burges was a colourful character who early in his career served as a colonel in the army, killed two men (one in a duel and one in a brawl), broke out of jail and received the king's pardon. Rather surprisingly, given this background, he was appointed as governor of Massachusetts Bay in 1715, although he never actually reached the region and resigned the following year.

Burges served as the British resident (a diplomatic agent ranking below an ambassador) in Venice on two occasions: between 1719 and 1721, and again between 1727 and his death there in 1736. This letter dates from that second appointment.

A key part of his role as resident was to keep the secretary of state in England informed of notable visitors to Venice. This was of particular interest to the British government at this time as James Francis Edward Stuart, the Old Pretender, was attracting Jacobites to his cause in Italy. Burges comments on some of the more notable visitors who were on their Grand Tours of Europe and points out that their lavish expenditure made them very popular on the continent, which was probably not in Britain's interests. Ironically, these visitors included a nephew of Henry Bourchier Fane (the man Burges had killed in a duel) and the twenty-year-old Earl Cowper (whose father had campaigned against the appointment of Burges as governor of Massachusetts Bay). The Venetian carnival celebrations, which were a particular draw to visitors, would run until Shrove Tuesday on 21 February 1730.

Burges also reported on some of the most notable Italian opera singers – the international celebrities of their day. Foremost among these was Carlo Maria Michelangelo Nicola Broschi, known as 'Farinelli', the famous castrato singer. Born in the south of Italy in 1705, he was already famous across Europe by 1730, recognised for the purity of his voice and its broad range. Francesca Cuzzoni (soprano), Francesco Bernardi – known as Senesino – (contralto castrato) and Faustina Bordoni (mezzo-

George Frideric Handel.

soprano) were already known in London, where they had performed in works of the composer George Frideric Handel to great acclaim. Despite their enthusiastic reception, though, Handel could not persuade Farinelli to join his company, although Farinelli's antipathy towards the English climate, which he feared would harm his voice, was overcome four years later in 1734 when he joined the 'Opera of the Nobility' in London, a rival to Handel's opera company.

This letter demonstrates the importance of continental culture to eighteenth-century Britain, exemplified by the diplomatic focus on the upper classes travelling through Europe to see and acquire cultural artefacts (many of which now feature in British museums and stately homes) and the visits of European performers to London in return.

Carlo Maria Michelangelo Nicola Broschi, or 'Farinelli'.

Venice, January y.e 20.th 1730. N.S.

My Lord

    I have been disabled of late from writing to your Grace
by a Humour that fell into my Right-Hand, which has given me more
Trouble than Pain: had there been more of y.e last in it, J should have
taken it for y.e Gout; but, not knowing what it was, J did nothing to it, and
in about six weeks time, it dispersed again, and went away, as it came,
of it self.

    We have now about Thirty of His Majesty's Subjects here, and
near Half that number has left us already to go on to Rome and to Naples.
When J was here formerly we seldom saw above eight or ten in a winter,
so much is y.e Humour of Travelling increased since that time: and as
most of y.e young Gentlemen that come abroad have money enough, they
spend it freely every where, which makes 'em well received, and may be
more for y.e honour of our Country, perhaps, than it is for her interest.
Lady Ferrers and her Brother S.r Richard Levinge, and a Son of Lord Gage's
of Ireland are of y.e number of those that have left us. Earl Cowper, Lord
Boyne, M.r Walpole, S.r Robert's 2.d Son, M.r Lyttleton, M.r Windham, S.r William
Morrice &c intend to stay here 'till towards y.e end of the Carnaval, and
then most of them are bound for Rome too.

    Farinello draws hither a great many Strangers to hear him.
the Virtuosi do all agree there never was such a Voice as his in y.e

world before: besides, he is young and a very good Figure upon ye Stage: but as he is engaged for three or four years to come, and, as I am told, has more than once express'd an unwillingness to go to England, for fear our Air should hurt his Voice, I can't tell whether your Grace will ever see him there or no. This is certain, When Mr Hendel was here last year, Farinello would never see him in particular, or ever returned him a Visit, tho' Mr Hendel was three times at his door to wait on him. The next best Voice in Italy is ye Cuzzoni, who sings better than ever she did, and, I think, has ye sweetest Pipe of ye Two. Senesino and Faustina are both at Turin, and are very well liked there; tho' I do assure your Grace, they could not maintain their Ground here last winter against Farinello alone. and we suffer not a little in ye opinion of this People, who pretend to be Souveraign Judges in Musick, for ye great Prices and Applauses we gave 'em in England.

Having no Business to trouble your Grace with at this time I give you this short account of our Company and Diversions, and am, with all duty and respect,

Your Grace's

most faithfull, most obedient
and most humble Servant

E Burges.

Venice, January the 20th 1730 NS

My Lord

    I have been disabled of late from writing to your Grace
by a Humour that fell into my Right Hand, which has given me more
trouble than Pain : had there been more of the last in it, I should have
taken it for the Gout; but, not knowing what it was, I did nothing to it, and
in about six weeks time, it dispersed again, and went away, as it came,
of itself.

    We have now about Thirty of His Majesty's Subjects here, and
near Half that number has left us allready to go on to Rome and to Naples.
When I was here formerly we seldom saw above eight or ten in a winter,
so much is the Humour of Travelling increased since that time : and as
most of the young Gentlemen that come abroad have money enough, they
spend it freely every where, which makes 'em well received, and may be
more for the honour of our Country, perhaps, than it is for her interest.
Lady Ferrers and her Brother S[i]r Richard Levinge, and a son of Lord Fane's
of Ireland are of the number of those that have left us. Earl Cowper, Lord
Boyne, Mr Walpole, S[i]r Robert's 2d son, Mr Littleton, Mr Windham, S[i]r William
Morrice &c intend to stay here 'till towards the end of the Carnaval, and
then most of them are bound for Rome too. Farinello draws hither a great many
strangers to hear him. The Virtuosi do all agree there never was such a Voice
as his in the

World before; besides, he is young and a very good Figure upon the stage
but as he is engaged for three or four years to come, and, as I am told,
has more than once express'd an unwillingness to go to England, for fear our
Air should hurt his Voice, I can't tell whether your Grace will ever see
him there or no. This is certain, When Mr Hendel was here last year,
Farinello would never see him in particular, or ever return'd him a
Visit, tho' Mr Hendel was three times at his door to wait on him. The
next best Voice in Italy is the Cuzzoni, who sings better than ever she
did, and, I think, has the sweetest Pipe of the Two. Senesino and Faustina
are both at Turin, and are very well liked there; tho', I do assure your
Grace, they could not maintain their Ground here last winter against
Farinello alone and we suffer not a little in the opinion of this People
who pretend to be souvereign Judges in Musick, for the /great/ Prices and Applauses we gave 'em in England.

Having no Business to trouble your Grace with at this time
I give you this short account of our Company and Diversions, and
am, with all duty and respect,

      Your Grace's

            most faithfull, most obedient
            and most humble Servant
                E Burges

An adventurous spirit
Charles Darwin accepts the position of naturalist on HMS *Beagle*

1 SEPTEMBER 1831

Charles Darwin's voyage on the *Beagle* has been described as one of the most important scientific expeditions in history. It provided an unparalleled opportunity to collect a wide range of plants and animals and to make scientific observations on the geology and topography of South America, and led to the theory of natural selection. The voyage was a key event in Darwin's life, but it almost never happened.

The story begins in June 1831 when the Admiralty commissioned HMS *Beagle*, a converted brig sloop with a crew of seventy-four, to undertake a hydrographic survey of South America. The *Beagle* was commanded by Captain Robert FitzRoy, a nephew of the Duke of Grafton. To support the expedition, FitzRoy sought to employ a naturalist and asked Francis Beaufort of the Admiralty Hydrographic Office if he could recommend a suitable candidate. Beaufort contacted his colleague George Peacock at Cambridge University, who in turn sought advice from his friend and professor of botany at Cambridge, the Reverend John Henslow. Their first choice was Leonard Jenyns, an avid beetle collector, and the curate of Swaffham Bulbeck in Cambridgeshire. Due to ill health and the demands of his parish, however, Jenyns declined the offer. Henslow then suggested the twenty-two-year-old Charles Darwin, whom he had taught at Cambridge.

Initially, Darwin also declined the offer: his father was opposed to it, he lacked the necessary experience of life at sea, and there was insufficient time to make preparations before the *Beagle* set sail in December 1831. Darwin's father considered the voyage a waste of time and wanted his son to settle down, but he eventually relented and on 1 September Darwin wrote an anxious letter to the Admiralty accepting the position – if it was still available – and apologising for the delay in responding.

Darwin had long wished to explore the flora and fauna of foreign lands and his request to join the expedition was soon approved on the condition that he was engaged in a private capacity and not as a member of the *Beagle*'s crew. This can be seen in the Admiralty's response to his letter scribbled in the bottom left-hand corner, which states: 'Let him be borne on the books for victualling only.'

The *Beagle* set sail from Devonport on 10 December 1831 and did not return home until October 1836. In the course of its five-year journey, the ship visited Brazil, Tierra del Fuego, Patagonia and the Galapagos Islands, allowing Darwin to collect a wide range of plants and animals. Over the next twenty years, Darwin sought to make sense of how the animal species he had seen during the voyage diversified and adapted to their surroundings. His findings were made known to the public in his famous book *On the Origin of Species by Means of Natural Selection*, published in 1859. The book proposed that animal populations evolve over generations via a process of natural selection and suggested that the diversity seen in the natural world arose by common descent through evolution.

Darwin spent the remainder of his life defending the theory of evolution against attacks from the Church and the religious establishment. He died in 1882 and is buried in Westminster Abbey. His book *On the Origin of Species* has been described as one of the most influential in human history.

Charles Darwin.

September the 1st

Shrewsbury

Sir

I take the liberty of writing to you
according to Mr. Peacocks desire to acquaint
you with my acceptance of the offer of going
with Capt. Fitzroy. Perhaps you may have
received a letter from Mr. Peacock stating
my refusals; this was owing to my Father
not at first approving of the plan, since
which time he has reconsidered the subject:
& has given his consent & therefore if the
appointment is not already filled up. — I
shall be very

happy to have the honor of accepting it.
— There has been some delay owing to my
being in Wales when the letter arrived. — I
set out for Cambridge tomorrow morning, to
see Professor Henslow: & from thence will
proceed immediately to London. —

    I remain Sir

        Your humble & obedient servant

           Chas. Darwin

Let him be borne on the books for
victualling only.

An artistic temperament
Lucian Freud's letter to Lilian Somerville

1954

This is the last of a series of correspondence written by Lucian Freud to Lilian Somerville – then director of the Fine Arts Department at the British Council and also part of the select committee (for the British collection) for the 1954 'La Biennale di Venezia', The Venice Biennial. At the time, Lilian was working with the commissioner, Sir Eric Maclagan, in organising the exhibition. The three previous letters in the collection discuss the Selection Committee's various decisions about Freud's paintings, but it is this final one that gives us a particular insight into the seeming anxiety and depression from which he was suffering.

Alongside Somerville, the British Selection Committee was made up of the elite of London's art world: John Rothenstein, Director of the Tate Gallery; Sir Philip Hendy, Director of the National Gallery; Herbert Read, founder of the ICA; and the artist and poet Roland Penrose.

In 1954, the British Pavilion showed paintings by fashionable young artists of the day, including Ben Nicholson, Francis Bacon, Henry Moore, the sculptor Reg Butler, and lithographers, such as Eduardo Paolozzi and Graham Sutherland. Lucian Freud was thirty-three at the time of the exhibition, which was to be his Venice debut.

Lucian Freud.

The exhibition, one of the most important in the world for artists' international careers, was also to be covered extensively by the British press. It was thus enormously important to Freud. The distress he felt about having some of his paintings rejected is apparent in his writing. He questions why, if they rejected so much of his work, they chose him at all. Not only did he think the rejected paintings were some of his 'better work', but he also felt they were representational of how he painted and, therefore, should be included.

Clearly Somerville and Maclagan's decisions seemed to differ from Freud's own strong personal views. The Committee would have had to make decisions often without the actual paintings being in front of them, relying for the most part on small black-and-white photographs. It is easy to see how difficult the debate must have been for both parties.

Freud suggests further changes and the possible addition of earlier works, but insists on the inclusion of his 'current painting', which was then unfinished. He thinks it will take a further three more weeks, but assures Somerville that it will be finished and adds that he will bring it to London as soon as it's dry.

Freud adds this final postscript to his correspondence, saying: 'It is hard to make further suggestions to the Committee, when the rejected paintings are less bad than others I have not yet suggested.'

'Less bad': it seems a sadly odd and a rather telling turn of phrase from a brilliant painter, who like many other brilliant artists throughout history was often beset by self-doubt while being at the same time emotionally driven.

The National Archives also holds a letter from Graham Sutherland, Freud's friend and co-exhibitor in Venice, written to Lilian Somerville regarding his own works. In his letter he also mentions Freud. He begins by saying it is none of his business, but feels he should mention that Lucian is rather worried about the selection of his paintings and the exclusion of certain ones that he feels are important. He (Freud) doesn't want to make demands, but he does feel that his best are not being included. Sutherland adds that, having seen them himself, he feels they would strongly 'augment the list' and for what it is worth should not be left out.

HOTEL LA LOUISIANE ★A

60, RUE DE SEINE, PARIS-6ᴱ

TÉL. : DANTON 97-08

ET ODÉON 10-86

—

No. 3.

Dear Lillian

I'm back in paris
and have just received
your letter of the 11th
I'm sorry about having removed
'Girl in bed' Here is
a photo of it. I am
anxious that 'girls head'
belonging to Cyreli
Connoly of Oak Cottage
Elmstead, nr. Ashford
should be included.
You told me the comittee
had rejected this pic-
ture on seing a bad

photograph of it.
Conolly's Phone number is
Elmstead 272 and he
is prepared to lend it.
So do please show them
the painting! Enclosed
also is a bad photo-
graph of the Berard
portrait. Perhaps after
the meeting you could
let me know what pain-
tings have so far been
decided on a

yours ever

Lucian

263

An artist enquires after the well-being of her work
Letter from Barbara Hepworth during the Festival of Britain

23 MARCH 1951

The artist and sculptor Barbara Hepworth was born in 1903, and trained as a sculptor at Leeds School of Art and the Royal College of Art in London. Her professional profile became increasingly established in the 1950s, such that her first public commissions for sculptures were for the Festival of Britain in 1951.

These sculptures included *Turning Forms* and *Contrapuntal Forms*, the former of which is mentioned in this letter, dated March 1951, within the contract files. In it, Hepworth confirms the delivery (and therefore completion) of *Turning Forms* to the festival site. The photograph of the sculpture shows it being placed by the Thameside Restaurant, Southbank, during the festival.

A contracted piece for the Festival of Britain authorities, the abstract sculpture was originally designed as a motor-driven sculpture that would turn at one revolution every two minutes. It now resides at Marlborough Science Academy, St Albans, as a static sculpture.

Sculpture was well represented at the Festival of Britain, with contributions from established artists such as Jacob Epstein. Other major and some lesser-known artists and designers also took part, creating work whose aim was to showcase British talent throughout the UK, with the centrepiece of the festival located on the South Bank, London.

Festival of Britain records created by the Festival of Britain Office and its predecessors is one of The National Archives' substantive collections related to art and design for the post-war period. As part of this, The National Archives holds records generated during the organisation of the events leading up to 1951. The Festival of Britain collection held here complements collections held in other archives, such as the Victoria and Albert Museum's Archive of Art and Design.

Hepworth working on *Contrapuntal Forms*, her
other commission for the Festival of Britain.

ref. C. 3/113

Trewyn Studio
St. Ives
Cornwall

Barbara Hepworth

FESTIVAL OF BRITAIN 1951
2 4 MAR 1951
CONTRACTS

23/3/51

The Director. Finance & Establishments.

dear Sir

My sculpture "Abstract Turning Forms" in re-inforced concrete was passed by Miss Jane Drew on Feb. 9th & delivered to the Festival site on Feb. 23rd. I understand that the next payment is due to me a month from this date & hope that you were notified of the delivery. Could you please inform me? I saw the architect & foreman in London a week ago on the site & as the base is not yet ready the sculpture is under a tarpaulin nearby, where a lot of rust & dirt is accumulating on it. This, I was assured, will be rectified

by a fresh coat of Snowcem when
the base is ready.
I am to visit the site on Friday
next week to supervise the
putting up of my large sculpture
near the dome, & will again
inspect "Turning Forms" which
is, I hope, covered by insurance
during this period of waiting until
the base is ready to have the
sculpture erected upon it?
Yours faithfully
Barbara Hepworth

23/3/51

The Director, Finance & Establishments.

Dear Sir

    My sculpture "Abstract Turning
Forms" in re-inforced concrete was
passed by Miss Jane Drew on Feb
9th & delivered to the Festival
site on Feb 23rd. I understand
that the next payment is due
to me a month from this date
and hope that you were notified
of the delivery. Could you please inform me?
I saw the architect & foreman in
London a week ago on the site
& as the base is not yet ready
the sculpture is under a tarpaulin
nearby where a lot of rust &
dirt is accumulating on it. This,
I was assured, will be rectified
by a fresh coat of snowcem when
the base is ready.
I am to visit the site on Friday
next week to supervise the
putting up of my large sculpture
near the dome & will again
inspect "Turning Forms" which
is, I hope, covered by insurance
during this period of waiting until
the base is ready to have the
sculpture erected upon it?

       Yours faithfully

        Barbara Hepworth

Barbara Hepworth preparing for the exhibition.

A scholarly prisoner and books from a friend
Nelson Mandela to Sir John Maud

14 SEPTEMBER 1962

Nelson Rolihlahla Mandela; 'Madiba'; 'The Father of South Africa'; leader of the African National Congress; Nobel Peace Prize winner and the first black head of state for South Africa, was once considered a Communist terrorist and violent revolutionary as he fought for the abolition of apartheid and for equality for all the people of South Africa.

Arrested in August 1962 for inciting illegal workers' strikes and for leaving the country without a passport, Mandela was remanded in custody in Johannesburg while awaiting trial. His campaigns were by now well-known across the globe, and he had gained sympathy and support from many corners.

Mandela's cause chimed with the socio-economic views and ideologies of the editor of the *Independent* newspaper in the UK, David Astor. The latter had voiced his support for the campaign against apartheid in South Africa and given support to the ANC. Working with the help of Sir John Maud, British Ambassador to South Africa, and Victor Verster, Commissioner of Prisons, Astor arranged for a number of books to be sent to Mandela, to aid in his 'intellectual growth' while he was imprisoned.

These history and sociology books were carefully chosen by Astor so as not to be seen as politically sensitive or representative of Communist views by the South African authorities, and were freely available from bookshops in the country. The titles sent on this occasion were: *A Short History of Africa* by Roland Oliver and JD Fage; *A History of Europe Vols. I and II* by HAL Fisher; *Essays in Biography* by JM Keynes; *Anatomy of Britain* by Anthony Sampson; and *The Making of the President 1960* by Theodore M White. Why he selected these particular books is unknown.

This simple gift, so painstakingly arranged by Astor and Maud, was clearly of huge importance to Mandela. However, this handwritten letter from Mandela thanking Maud for 'making it possible' for him to receive the books shows that he did not know who the 'friend' in England who sent the books was, but he was nevertheless incredibly grateful for the present and, reading between the lines, the thought that went into it. Astor had not made it known that he was Mandela's benefactor at this point, and it would not be until years later, after many more books had been sent and Mandela had been released from prison, that the two men would meet and continue their friendship in person.

Below Mandela's signature on this letter are the words 'Awaiting Trial Prisoner', along with his prisoner number. The handwriting looks different to Mandela's cursive script in the main letter, and its origins could point to a wish by the prison to somehow negate Mandela's identity and political persona and to simply reduce him to the status of a numbered inmate.

Astor and Maud would go on to send more books to Mandela while he was in custody, and to later support and arrange for him to study for a full law degree in correspondence with the University of London while he was imprisoned for life in Robben Island after the Rivonia Trial.

Nelson Mandela.

September 10, 1962

I have marked this note "Personal" because it deals
with a point on which you kindly gave me your personal
advice when I asked you for it when you were leaving my
house a few weeks ago.

A friend of mine in England had asked me whether he
could send books to a South African prison for the use of
Nelson Mandela, who he understood to be awaiting trial.
You told me about the regulations applying to such cases
and kindly said that if I sent the books to you you would
arrange for them to be forwarded if they were unobjectionable.

My friend has now sent me, through Van Schaik's
Bookshop in Pretoria, the following books:

A Short History of Africa	Roland Oliver and J.D. Fage
A History of Europe, Volumes I and II	H.A.L. Fisher
Essays in Biography	J.M. Keynes
Anatomy of Britain	Anthony Sampson
The Making of the President	Theodore H. White

It would be so kind of you if you could transmit these
to whatever the prison is in which Nelson Mandela is confined.
The books are all new copies and are freely available in
South Africa; so that I hope there will be no objection to
their transmission.

With my warm thanks,

V.R. Verster Esq.,
  The Commissioner of Prisons,
    157 Schoeman Street,
      Pretoria.

JOHANNESBURG PRISON.

13.9.62

THE COMMISSIONER OF PRISONS,
P R E T O R I A.

Dear Sir,

    I acknowledge with thanks receipt of the
following books :-

        A Short History of Africa by Roland Oliver and
                         J.D. Fage.
        A History of Europe (Vol. I and II) by
                         H.A.L. Fisher.
        Essays in Biography by J.M. Keynes.
        Anatomy of Britain by Anthony Sampson.
        The Making of the President by Theodore H. White.

Yours faithfully,

N Mandela

13/9/62

The Jail
Johannesburg
14th September 1962

Sir John Maud, G.C.B., C.B.E.,
The British Embassy.
No. 6. Hill Street.
Pretoria.

Dear Sir,

I have received the six
books which were sent to me by
a friend in England through
your Embassy.

I thank you for making it
possible for me to receive them,
and I should be grateful if
you would kindly inform the
friend, should you be in possession
of his or her address, that I
greatly appreciate this valuable
present.

yours faithfully
Mandela.
NELSON MANDELA.
AWAITING TRIAL PRISONER
13260/62.

The Jail

Johannesburg

14th September 1962

Sir John Maud GCB, CBE

The British Embassy

No 6 The Street

Pretoria

Dear Sir

 I have received the six
books which were sent to me
by a friend in England through
your Embassy.

 I thank you for making
it possible for me to receive
them, and I should be grateful
if you would kindly inform
the friend, should you be
in possession of his or
her address, that I greatly
appreciate this valuable
present.

 Yours faithfully
  N Mandela
 NELSON MANDELA
 AWAITING TRIAL PRISONER
 13260/62

A widow's appeal to 'bring Dylan home'
Letter from Caitlin Thomas to local authorities

OCTOBER 1955

'And death shall have no dominion', Dylan Thomas wrote; and it appears he was right.

The Swansea-born poet died aged just thirty-nine while on a lecture tour of the USA. He was brought home and laid to rest in an extended section of Laugharne Parish Church graveyard with nothing but a modest white cross to mark the spot. Two years later, in October 1955, his widow, Caitlin Thomas, wrote to the authorities, unhappy that this place was not fitting for 'Wales' foremost poet'.

Caitlin, who was by then living in Italy, had returned to the South Wales fishing village of Laugharne but was dismayed that she 'could not even distinguish which was [his]' grave as it had 'been completely ignored by his own townspeople'.

According to her, a more suitable resting place for her late husband would be the garden of their Boathouse home where, in his writing shed, Dylan had crafted some of his most famous works, including part of *Under Milk Wood*. There, Caitlin could tend his grave away from the 'bleak extension' of the church cemetery.

In her handwritten letter, Caitlin explained how at the time of Dylan's death in a New York hotel on 9 November 1953 she had been more concerned with getting him home to Wales than with his final resting place. Now, however, she wrote: 'I should feel much happier if he were facing the water that he loved and wrote about in his poems' rather than the 'desolate spot' in the overspill of St Martin's where he lay.

The application to exhume the poet's body and reinter it at the Boathouse came to the attention of the press, with *The Times*, *Daily Herald* and *Manchester Guardian* being among the publications to carry the story of Caitlin's application to 'bring Dylan home'.

Caitlin's appeal was accompanied by a letter to the Home Office from her solicitors stating: 'The grave is frequently visited by people and particularly by Americans on holiday in this country', and who said it would have been 'preferable' had he been buried at the Boathouse 'where a very suitable site exists'.

There were no objections from Carmarthen Rural District Council's Public Health Department and no legal objections from the Home Office.

However, the vicar of Laugharne, Reverend Victor H Jones, wrote to the Home Office to say there was 'much to be said against the proposed removal', which was 'outside [his] spiritual direction', although it would be up to the bishop of the diocese to consecrate any new burial ground. Dylan's mother, Florence, was also reportedly 'very concerned' at Caitlin's proposals.

In their response, the Home Office wrote to say a licence would be granted to exhume the poet's body and reinter him at the Boathouse on the payment of a £2 fee. However, it is not clear whether the fee was ever paid, as sixty years later Dylan's grave remains in the churchyard in Laugharne. Caitlin was buried alongside him following her own death in 1994.

Dylan Thomas and his wife, Caitlin.

Dylan is a very exceptional person, and Wales' foremost poet; and I think the place where he is buried is not worthy of him. I think that he deserves to be put appart, in a special place of his own, that is both near to him, and does him honour as a poet for future generations.

I went up to see his grave a little time ago, and I could not even distinguish which was his; and the careful orders I had given, before going to Italy, to have it planted with continual flowers, and always kept tidy, had been completely ignored by his own towns people.

So, rather than put up a stone, or some distinguishing mark of love and respect, in that desolate spot; I should feel much happier if he was facing the water, that he loved and wrote about in his poems, and close to me where we lived together.

2 The reason I did not object before to his place of burial, was that I thought only of getting him back from America to Wales; and I imagined he would be buried in the old church-yard. I had no idea, till the day of the funeral, that he was being buried in that bleak extension of it; and I was in no fit state to object then.

If the grave is in the Boathouse Garden, I shall be able to tend it myself, and see that it is kept as I should like it to be kept. And when my time comes to join him, I hope to be buried alongside him.

Caitlin Thomas
Boathouse
Laugharne

Dylan is a very exceptional person, and Wales foremost poet; and I think the place where he is buried is not worthy of him. I think that he deserves to be put appart, in a special place of his own, that is both dear to him and does him honour as a poet for future generations.

I went up to see his grave a little time ago, and I could not even distinguish which was his; and the careful orders I had given, before going to Italy, to have it planted with continual flowers, and always kept tidy, had been completely ignored by his own townspeople.

So, rather than put up a stone, or some distinguishing mark of love and respect, in that desolate spot; I should feel much happier if he was facing the water, that he loved and wrote about in his poems, and close to me where we lived together.

The reason I did not object before to his place of burial was that I thought only of getting him back from America to Wales; and I imagined he would be buried in the old churchyard. I had no idea, till the day of the funeral, that he was being buried in that bleak extension of it; and I was in no fit state to object then.

If the grave is in the Boathouse Garden, I shall be able to tend it myself, and see that it is kept as I should like it to be kept. And when my time comes to join him, I hope to be buried alongside him.

        Caitlin Thomas
            Boathouse
                Laugharne

The Thomases' beloved boathouse at Laugharne.

Beatles' 'peerage' makes waves in Mexico
Letter from the Foreign Office to the British Embassy in Mexico

24 JUNE 1965

The Fab Four and the official archive of the UK government: these are not two phrases you would necessarily expect to see in the same sentence. However, as the collection of The National Archives contains documents relating to interactions of citizens with the government and authorities, it is only natural that many celebrities should appear in the records.

This letter is just one of a number of documents at The National Archives charting the rise of The Beatles. Many are reports from diplomats around the globe sent back to the Foreign Office in London, detailing the local reaction to visits to other countries by John, Paul, George and Ringo. Others are letters, like this example from the British Embassy in Mexico from June 1965, dealing with specific events relating to The Beatles.

This letter explores the reaction of the Mexican people to the award of MBEs to the members of the band. A mistaken notion that this meant The Beatles had been elevated to the peerage had led to a slew of letters of complaint from members of the public in Mexico. It is not only interesting because of the subjects of its content, but also because of the author and recipient. NJA Cheetham, who wrote the letter, was in fact the British ambassador to Mexico. Many records relating to his official career can be found in The National Archives and show the key role he played in European politics and diplomatic relations following the Second World War and into the 1950s. The recipient, meanwhile, was Richard Mercer Keene Slater, who went on to become the British high commissioner to Uganda and, in 1972, was famously expelled from the country by Idi Amin.

It says a lot about the astounding international fame of The Beatles that they provoked this response and that diplomats at such a high level felt the need to write back to the Foreign Office on the reaction of locals across the globe. It is fascinating to think that the four young lads from Liverpool could cause such a fuss that officials thought it might damage international relations.

The Beatles.

(ID 1677/4/65)

British Embassy,

Mexico City

24 June, 1965

Dear Dick,

It is perhaps not/surprising that the award of the
M.B.E. to the Beatles should have attracted a fair amount
of publicity. But in Mexico it has given rise to an
inordinate amount of comment in the press. Indeed it is
no exaggeration to say that it has been a major topic here
recently.

2.   Unfortunately most of the local comment has been adverse,
and this has been particularly true of the serious newspapers. Several cartoonists have seized the opportunity to
poke fun at us and one newspaper asked in a headline if the
English had gone mad. Other commentators have delved into
the past and have sought to compare the Beatles' award to
the titles bestowed on "the English pirates" (Drake, Hawkins,
etc.) in the old days. The consensus, with few exceptions,
is that the award is a sign of British decadence. I have
also received a few anonymous letters to that effect. It is
particularly regrettable that one or two writers have gone
so far as to criticize the Queen personally, which is most
unusual because the Mexicans are normally very respectful
of the dignity of the Royal Family.

3.   I think that much of the criticism stems from the fact
that the Mexicans have the misguided notion that the Beatles
have been elevated to the Peerage! Press commentators have
said that they are now "nobles", while cartoonists have
wrapped them in ermine-trimmed capes. To correct this mis-
conception and put the matter in its right perspective, I

/wrote

R. M. K. Slater, Esq., C.M.G.,
        American Department,
            Foreign Office,
                London, S.W.1.

wrote to all the important newspapers explaining the significance of the award. Most of them have published my
letter.

4.   Lately, and particularly since Prince Philip's visit
last October, our relations with the press have been
friendly and they have treated us well. It is a pity
that we are now being criticized and even ridiculed in
this way. I can only hope that the storm will blow over
soon and that it will not cause any lasting damage to
the British image in Mexico.

Your ever,
John

(N. J. A. Cheetham)

Hounding the Home Office on TV censorship
Mary Whitehouse to Harold Wilson

19 JULY 1966

The National Viewers' and Listeners' Association (VALA) was publicly launched in 1965 with the intent of making sure that the public – who, at the time, paid £67,000,000 in yearly licence fees – had a say in the maintenance of standards across broadcasting. A leaflet produced by the body, whose Hon General Secretary was Mrs Mary Whitehouse, stated that the VALA fought for 'responsibility – not censorship' as they believed that the effects of television policy could be traced through society. 'Why,' they asked, 'do advertisers pay enormous sums of money for a minute on television if they are not convinced that people are affected by what they see?'

Mary Whitehouse wrote many letters to the Home Office in an attempt to get the government to change things in the television industry, in addition to running campaigns and producing opinion surveys. One survey produced in 1967 asked viewers to comment on six recent programmes they had watched over a three-month period, including the date and service each show had aired on, and how they dealt with topics such as womanhood, family life, sex and authority.

She was particularly concerned with the BBC, which she believed had adopted 'an arrogant and patronising attitude towards its viewers' that was far more concerned with the rights of young playwrights than with the community as a whole. Some of the content Mary Whitehouse was keen to curtail included the use of particular 'four-letter words' and a presenter's 'highly emotive' anti-Americanism in a programme about the Vietnam War that aired on BBC1.

Staff at the Home Office soon began to tire of her relentless letters as there was little that they felt they could do to intervene. 'It is the Chairman and other Governors of the BBC who are responsible for the content and timing of the programme broadcast' explained one tired civil servant in response to her telegram about the coarse language used in a television series called *Till Death Us Do Part*.

Mary Whitehouse

Such responses, however, only prompted Mary Whitehouse to make a more personalised appeal to the prime minister to use television as a platform for curing 'national malaise' by circulating ideas about how productivity and cooperation could be improved. In a letter written to Harold Wilson in July 1966 she wrote: 'Is it not vitally important, facing as we do, an economic Dunkirk, that the whole resources of industry should be mobilised in this way, and that the broadcasting of this wealth of ideas should be made a priority?'

NATIONAL VIEWERS' AND LISTENERS' ASSOCIATION

NATIONAL
VALA

Chairman: J. BARNETT, ESQ.,
Chief Constable, Lincolnshire.

Hon. Treasurer:
H. COBDEN TURNER, ESQ., J.P.
M.Inst.C.E., M.I.E.E., M.I.Mech.E.,
89, Oxford Street,
Manchester, 1.

Hon. General Secretary:
MRS. MARY WHITEHOUSE,
The Wold, Claverley,
Wolverhampton.
Tel. Claverley 375.

19/7/66.

The Rt. Hon. Harold Wilson. M.P.
The Prime Minister.

Dear Sir,

Dear Sir, Realising something of the tremendous burden which lies upon your shoulders at this time, we seek this opportunity of bringing to your notice the part we feel broadcasting could play in the resolving of our present difficulties.

It could provide a platform for the ordinary men and women of both labour and management to put across to the whole country their ideas and experience on how productivity can be increased and a new spirit of co-operation be developed.

The World Cup was considered important enough for all our viewing to be organised around it. Is it not vitally important,facing as we do, an economic Dunkirk,that the whole resources of industry should be mobilised in this way,and that the broadcasting of this wealth of ideas should be made a priopity?

If, alongside programmes of this kind,a general policy could be established in which,directly and indirectly,it is shewn that enery is largely dependent on clean living,that reliability and co-operation are marketable qualities,and that mutual responsibility is the hall mark of moral as well as economic solvency,then television could play an immediate and most significant part in curing our national malaise.

This present crisis is television's golden opportunity to prove its capacity for active and positive good.

Yours sincerely,

Mary Whitehouse.

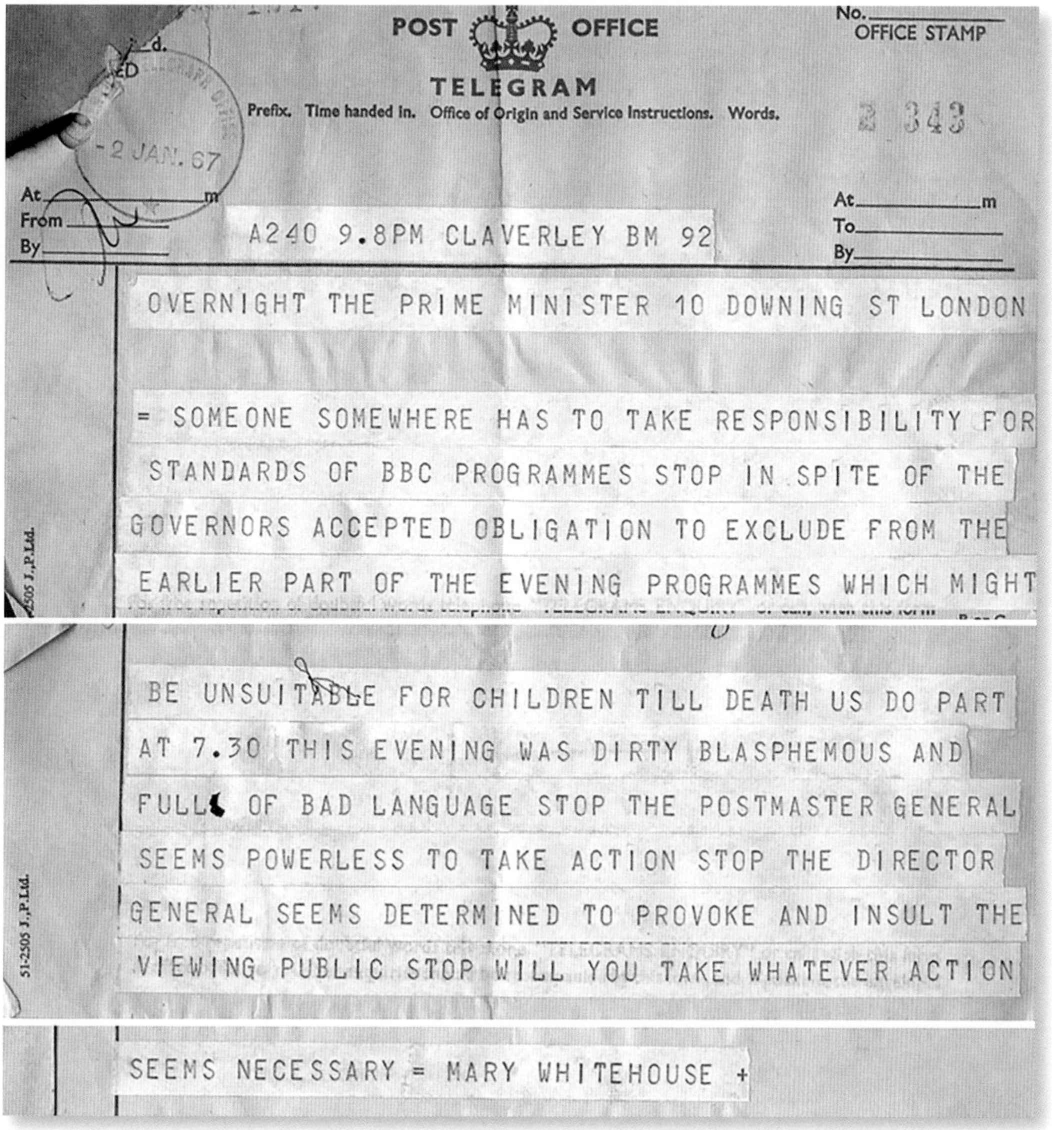

POST OFFICE

TELEGRAM

Prefix. Time handed in. Office of Origin and Service Instructions. Words.

No.
OFFICE STAMP

2 343

- 2 JAN. 67

At m
From
By

A240 9.8PM CLAVERLEY BM 92

At m
To
By

OVERNIGHT THE PRIME MINISTER 10 DOWNING ST LONDON

= SOMEONE SOMEWHERE HAS TO TAKE RESPONSIBILITY FOR STANDARDS OF BBC PROGRAMMES STOP IN SPITE OF THE GOVERNORS ACCEPTED OBLIGATION TO EXCLUDE FROM THE EARLIER PART OF THE EVENING PROGRAMMES WHICH MIGHT BE UNSUITABLE FOR CHILDREN TILL DEATH US DO PART AT 7.30 THIS EVENING WAS DIRTY BLASPHEMOUS AND FULL OF BAD LANGUAGE STOP THE POSTMASTER GENERAL SEEMS POWERLESS TO TAKE ACTION STOP THE DIRECTOR GENERAL SEEMS DETERMINED TO PROVOKE AND INSULT THE VIEWING PUBLIC STOP WILL YOU TAKE WHATEVER ACTION SEEMS NECESSARY = MARY WHITEHOUSE +

51-2505 J.,P.Ltd.

Index

Project coordinators
Timothy Cross • Ela Kaczmarska • Hester Vaizey

Contributors
Louise Bell • Jessamy Carlson • Ann Chow • Dr. Sean Cunningham • Chris Day
Sarah Dellar • Dr. Juliette Desplat • Dr. Daniel Gilfoyle • Kathryn Fox • Andrew Harrison
Rachel Hillman • Clare Horrie • Sally Hoult • Sally Hughes • Iqbal Husain
Juliette Johnstone • Ela Kaczmarska • Roger Kershaw • Dr. Katy Mair • Keith Mitchell Dr.
Jessica Nelson • Caroline Osborne-James • Bruno Pappalardo • Mark Pearsall Ruth
Selman • Ralph Thompson • Benjamin Trowbridge • Dr. Stephen Twigge   Carianne
Whitworth • Marianne Wilson

With thanks to
Paul Johnson • Linda Stewart

SOURCES FOR LETTERS AND IMAGES

The National Archives
Drunkenness, debauchery and dark dealings: 14–19: CN 28/1, COPY 1/23, J 90/1225;
20–23: COPY 1/494, HO 144/1205/222030; **24–27:** HO 190/231; 28–31: HO 45/11968;
32–35: WORK 16/543; **36–41:** CRIM 1/2747

Politics and power: 44–47: C 66/2; **48–51:** C 81/1392, DL 10/392 (Duchy of Lancaster
copyright material in The National Archives is reproduced by permission of the Chancellor
and Council of the Duchy of Lancaster); **52–55:** SP 1/121; **56–61:** SP 8/1, T 40/1D; **62–69:**
MPF 1/2, SP 54/26/32; **70–71:** HO 144/21627; **72–77:** DO 142/484, EXT 11/145; **78–81:** CO
876/88, INF 14/19; **82–85:** FO 371/42809, INF 1/244; **86–89:** PREM 19/2577; **90–93:** PREM
19/3213

Expeditions, foreign policy and espionage: 96–101: CO 2/20; **102–107:** COPY 1/1, FO
95/722; **108–111:** WO 32/6350; **112–115:** FO 383/15, KV 2/822; **116–119:** HW 1/6, HW 25/3;
120–123: PREM 16/292; **124–127:** HS 9/836/5; **128–129:** PREM 19/1647; **130–133:** PREM
19/3002

Conflict, unrest and protest: 136–139: COPY 1/142, SP 12/213; **140–145:** SP 9/245/11, SP
16/511/43, SP 63/281; **146–151:** PRO 30/55/58/38; **152–159:** ADM 1/408/97; **160–163:** HO
52/8; **164–175:** WO 32/5110, WO 95/4272; **176–179:** HO 45/10804/308532; **180–183:** WO
339/51440; **184–187:** FO 371/33035, WO 208/1768; **188–193:** KV 4/259, PREM 4/43a/9; **194–
199:** HO 207/386, HO 287/469; **200–207:** AIR 40/277, CO 980/79, CO 1047/741

Relations and relationships: 210–213: SP 10/2; **214–219:** E 30/1470; **220–223:** KB
27/1289/2, SP 12/215; **224–231:** PCOM 8/434; **232–239:** HO 144/1118/203442; **240–245:** HO
302/11; **246–257:** PREM 11/1565

Art, science and popular culture: 260–265: SP 99/63; **266–269:** ADM 1/4541; **270–273:**
BW 2/599; **274–279:** WORK 25/201, WORK 25/259/G2/C3/113; **280–285:** DO 119/1478;
286–291: HO 282/11; **292–295:** FO 371/187127; **296–299:** HO 256/719

Images from other sources

12 Guildhall Library & Art Gallery/Heritage Images/Getty Images; **37** Hulton-Deutsch Collection/CORBIS/Corbis via Getty Images; **42** Hulton Archive/Getty Images; **44** Popperfoto/Getty Images; **45** Hulton Archive/Getty Images; **52** Fine Art Images/ Heritage Images/Getty Images; **53** Fine Art Images/Heritage Images/Getty Images; **62** The Print Collector/Print Collector/Getty Images; **72** Universal History Archive/ Getty Images; **77** Universal History Archive/UIG via Getty Images; **78** Popperfoto/ Getty Images); **79** Daily Herald Archive/SSPL/Getty Images; **86** Bettmann/Getty Images; **87** Tim Graham/Getty Images; **90** Jean GUICHARD/Gamma-Rapho via Getty Images; **91** Peter Turnley/Corbis/VCG via Getty Images; **92** Popperfoto/Getty Images; **96** Hulton Archive/Getty Images; **102** National Archive/Newsmakers/Getty Images; **107** The Cartoon Collector/Print Collector/Getty Images; **108** London Stereoscopic Company/Getty Images; **112** adoc-photos/Corbis via Getty Images; **120** Photo12/UIG via Getty Images; **126** Laski Diffusion/Getty Images; 130 Bettmann/Getty Images; **133** Owen Franken/Corbis via Getty Images; **134** Fine Art Images/Heritage Images/ Getty Images; **136** Fine Art Images/Heritage Images/Getty Images; **146** Universal History Archive/UIG via Getty Images; **152** National Galleries Of Scotland/Getty Images; **161** Classic Image / Alamy Stock Photo; 176 Hulton-Deutsch Collection/ CORBIS/Corbis via Getty Images; **181** Hulton Archive/Getty Images; **185** Victor Temin/Slava Katamidze Collection/Getty Images; **208** Universal History Archive/Getty Images; **211** Universal History Archive/Getty Images; **225** Universal History Archive/ Getty Images; **240** Hulton-Deutsch Collection/CORBIS/Corbis via Getty Images; **246** Keystone/Getty Images; **247** Paul Popper/Popperfoto/Getty Images; **257** Popperfoto/Getty Images; **258** John Pratt/Keystone/Getty Images; **260** Fine Art Images/Heritage Images/Getty Images; **261** Peter Horree / Alamy Stock Photo; **267** Universal History Archive/Getty Images; **270** Paul Popper/Popperfoto/Getty Images; **279** Hulton-Deutsch Collection/CORBIS/Corbis via Getty Images; **281** API/ Gamma-Rapho via Getty Images; **287** Culture Club/Getty Images; **291** Terence Spencer/The LIFE Picture Collection/Getty Images; **293** Fotos International/Getty Images; **296** Les Lee/Express/Getty Images; **297** Central Press/Getty Images.